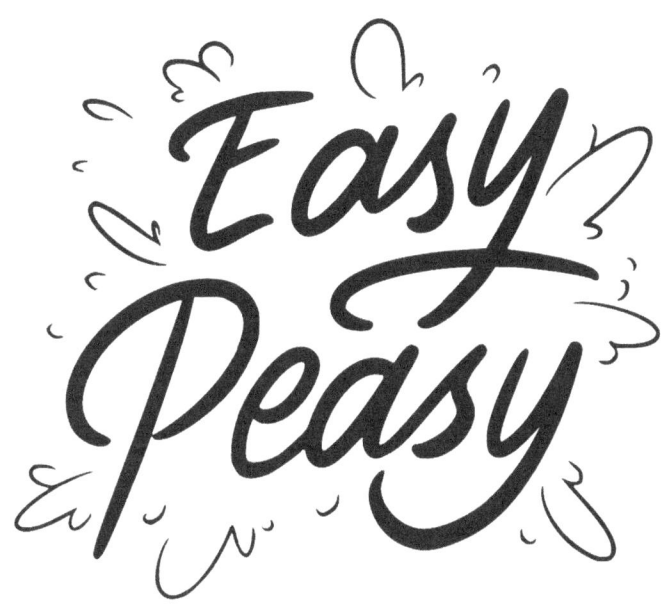

COLORING

BOOK FOR

ANYONE

Copyright © 2022 Trina L Conner

All rights reserved.

No part of this book may be reproduced,

stored in a retrieval system or transmitted by any means

without the written permission of the author.

ISBN: 9798371672643

Independently published

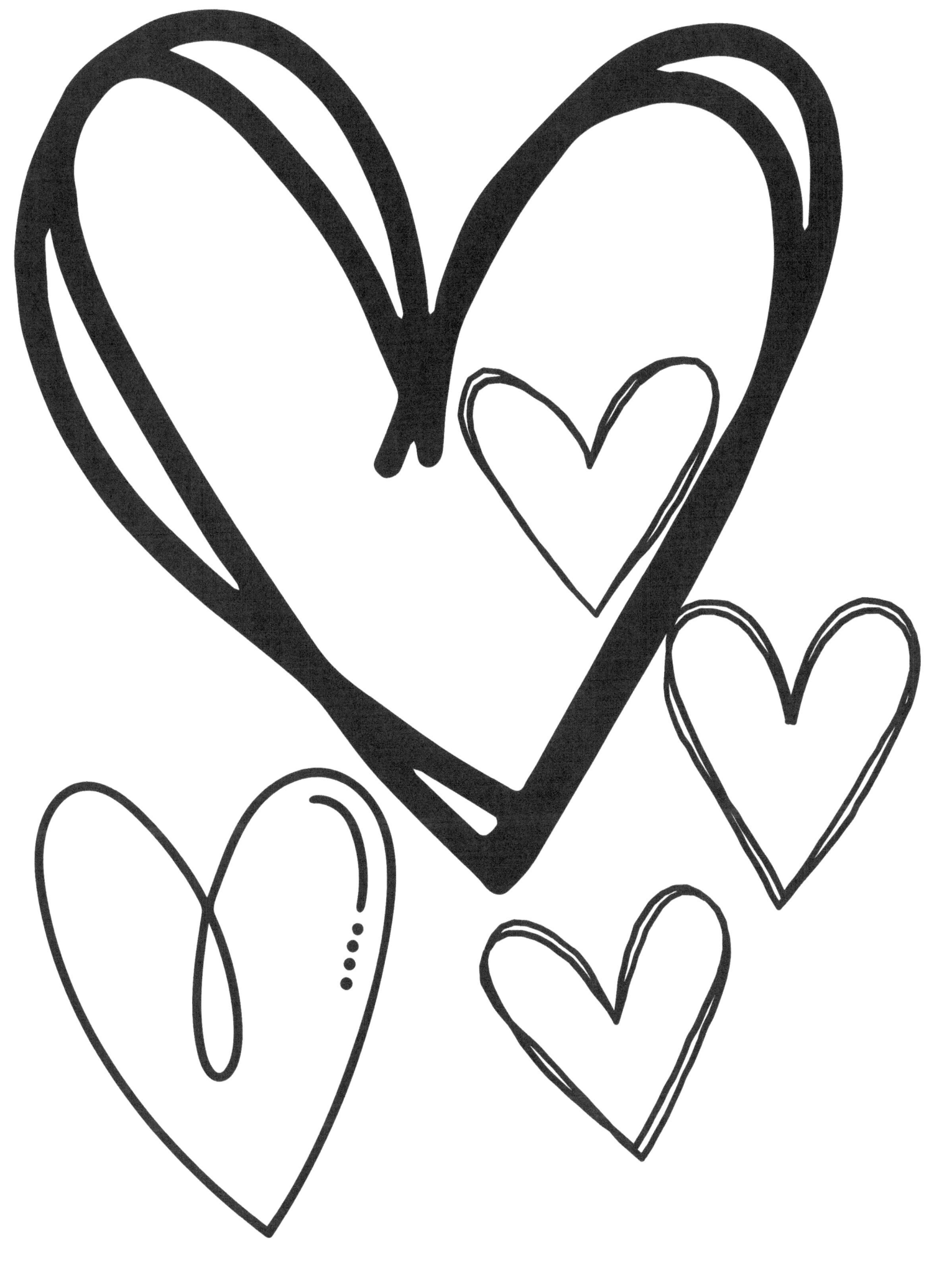

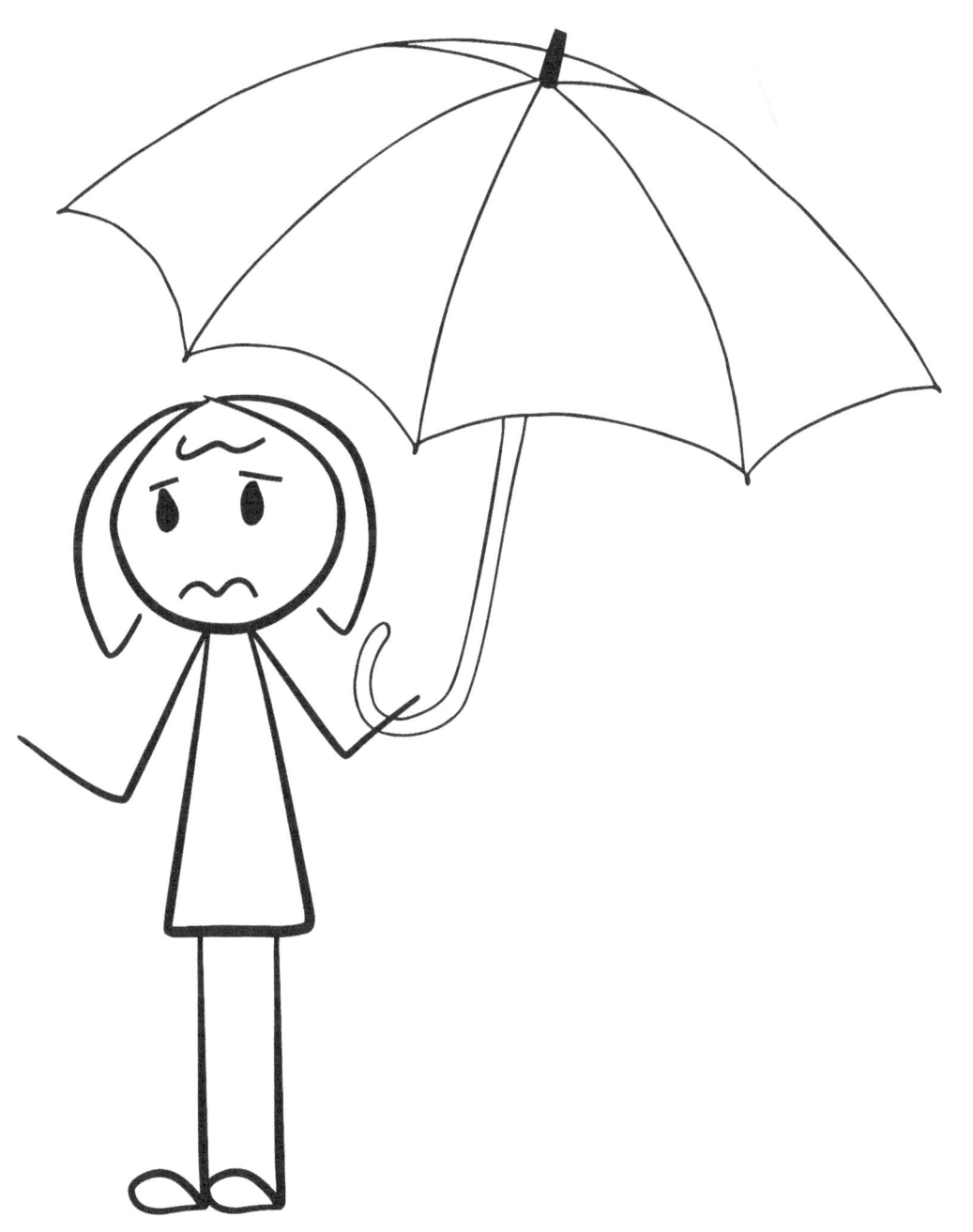

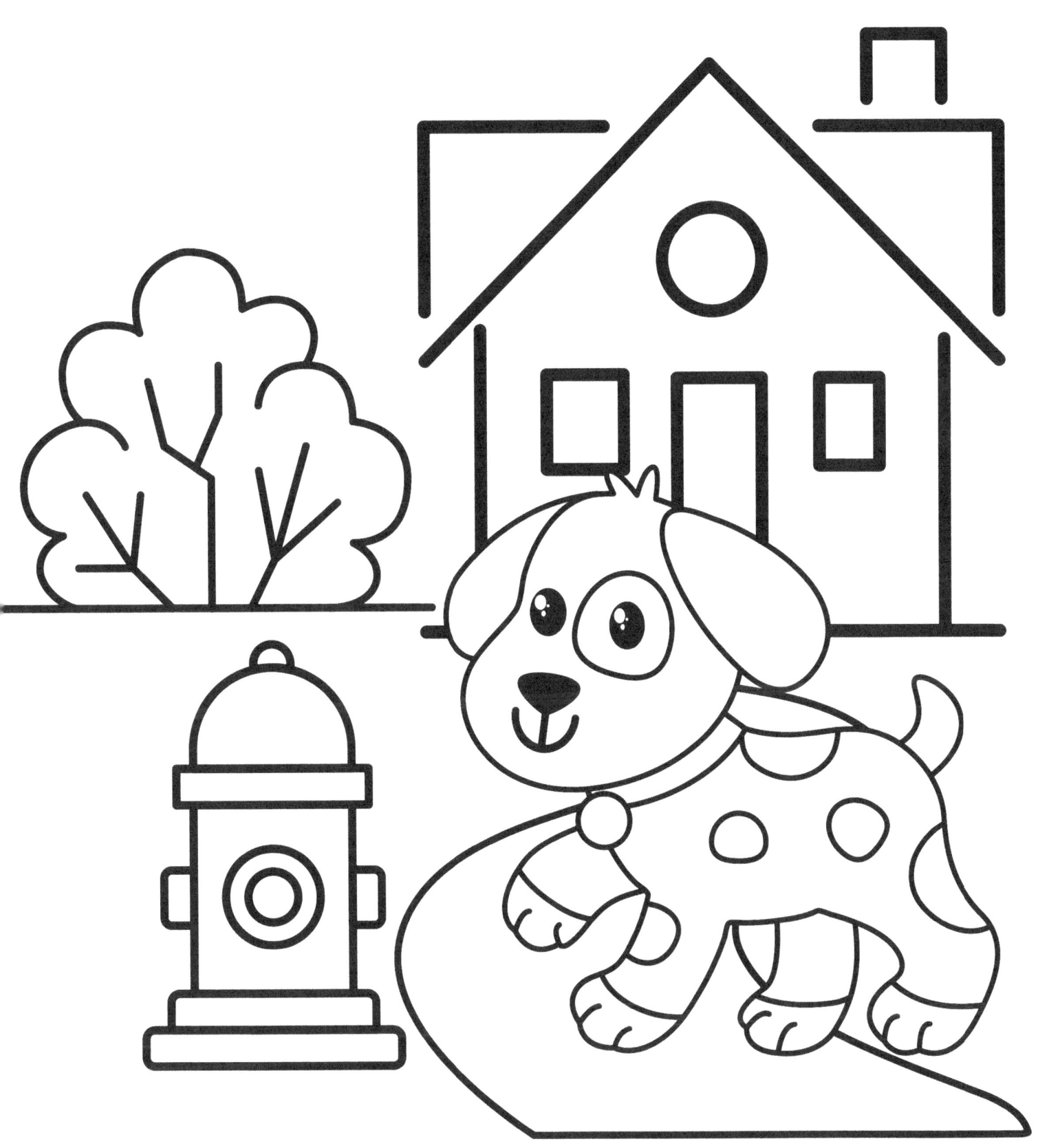

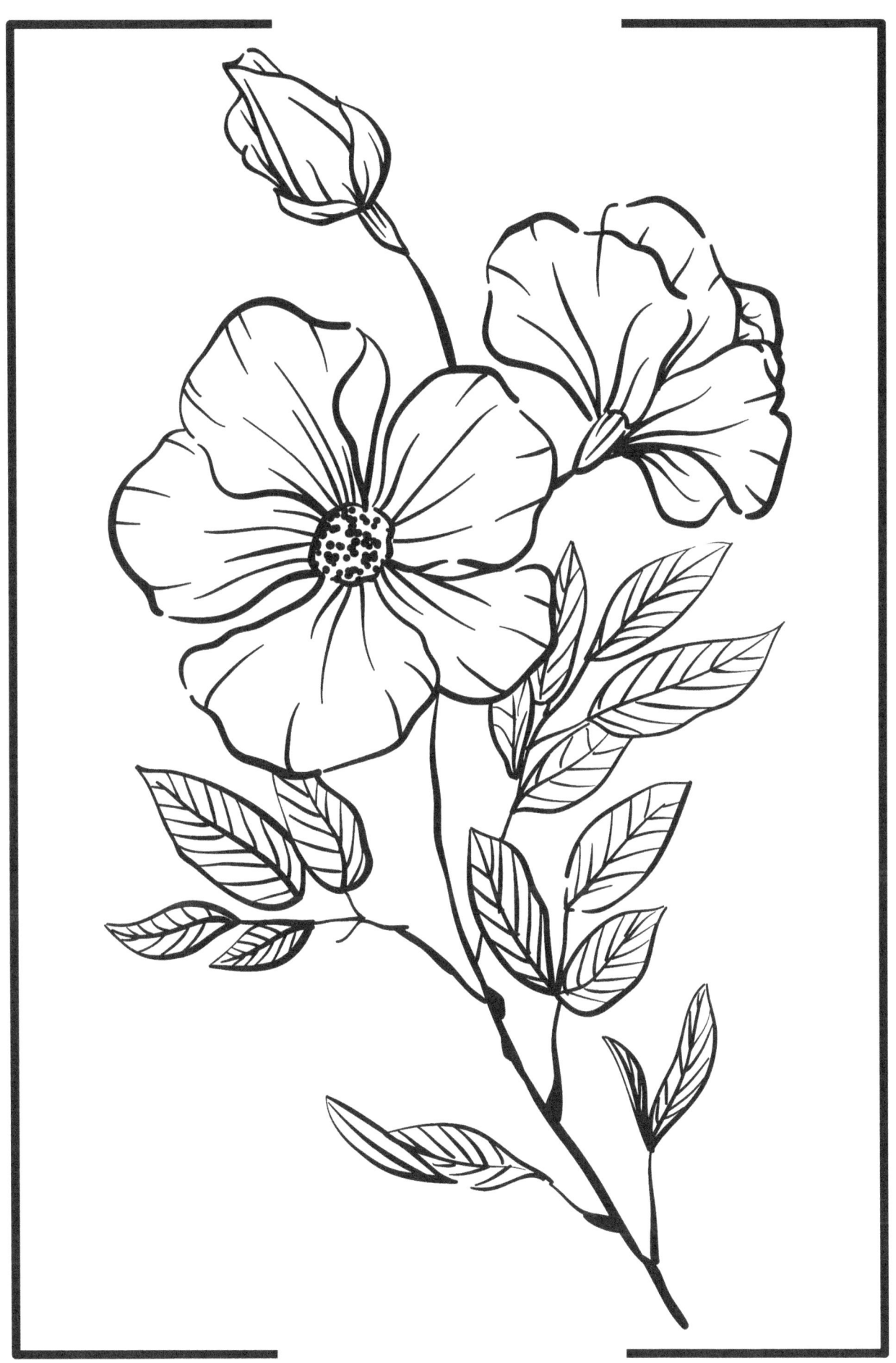

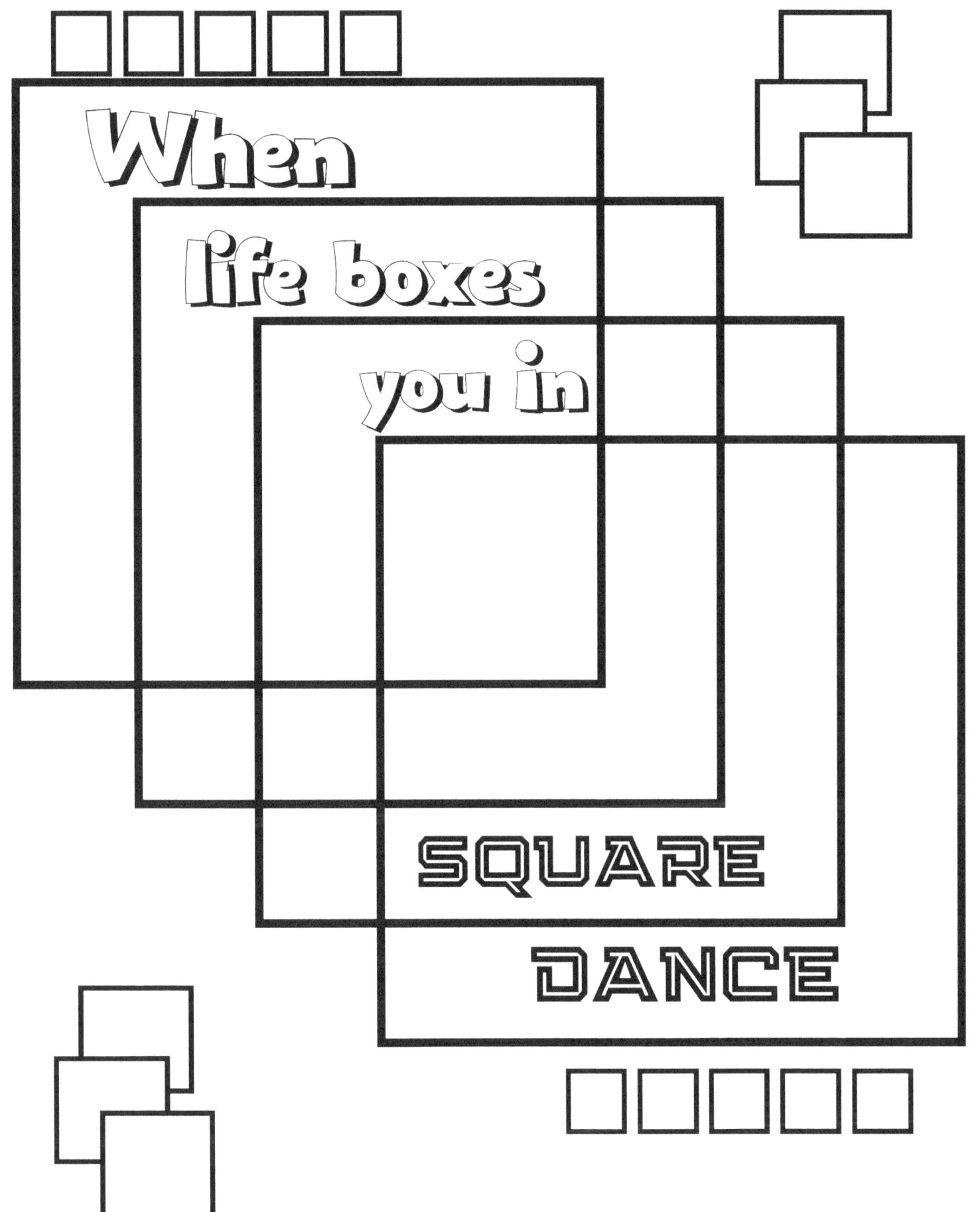

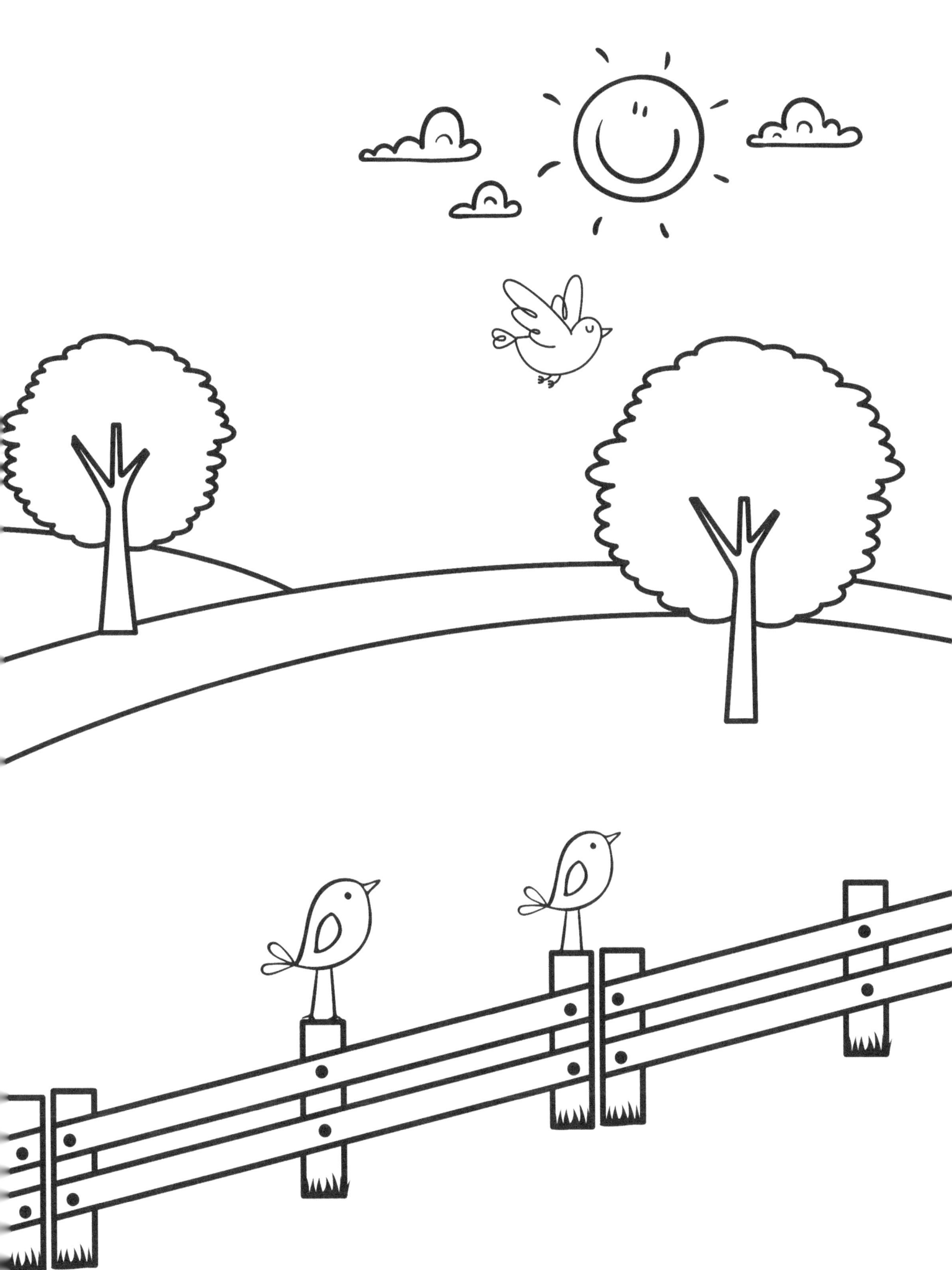

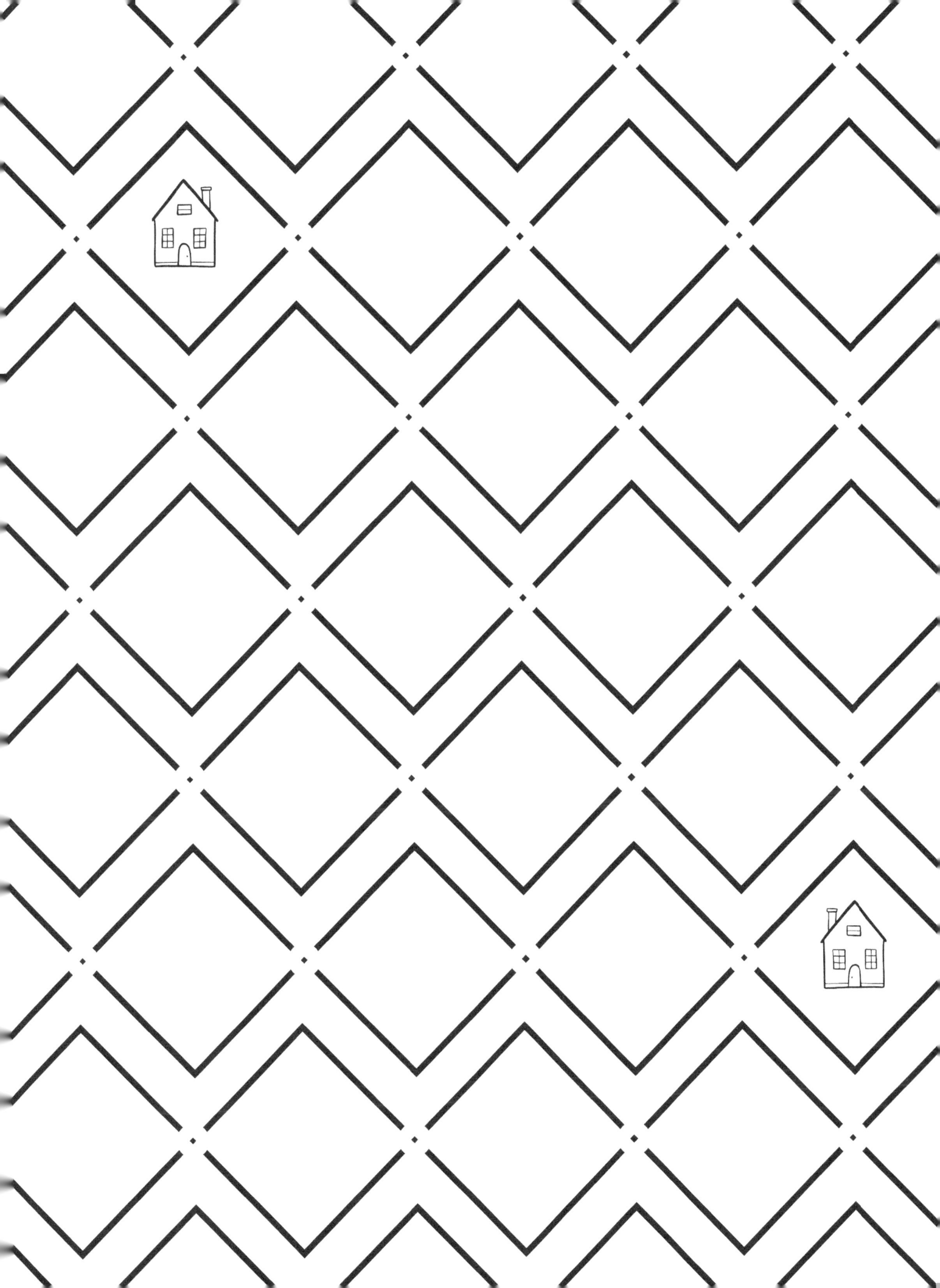

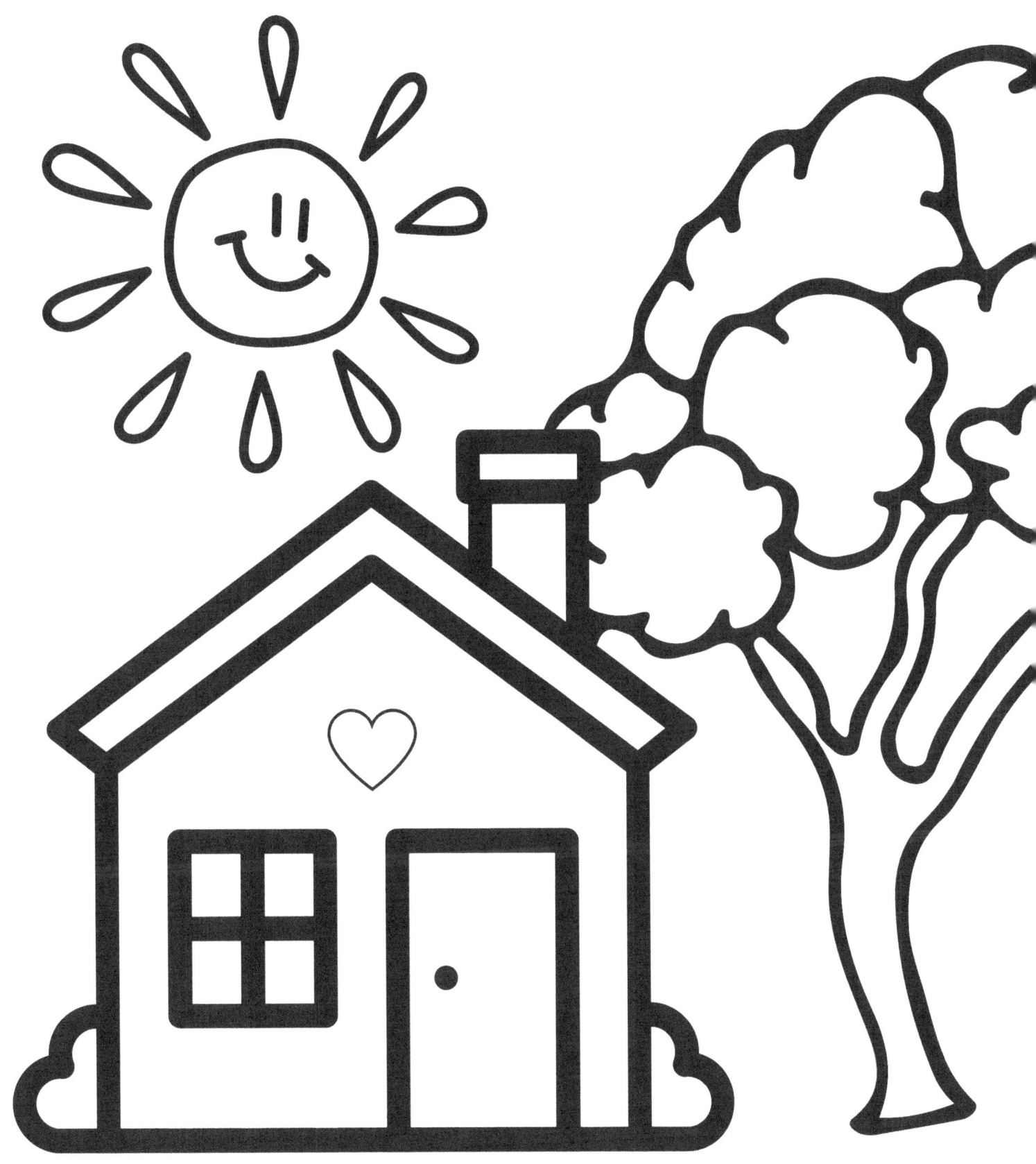

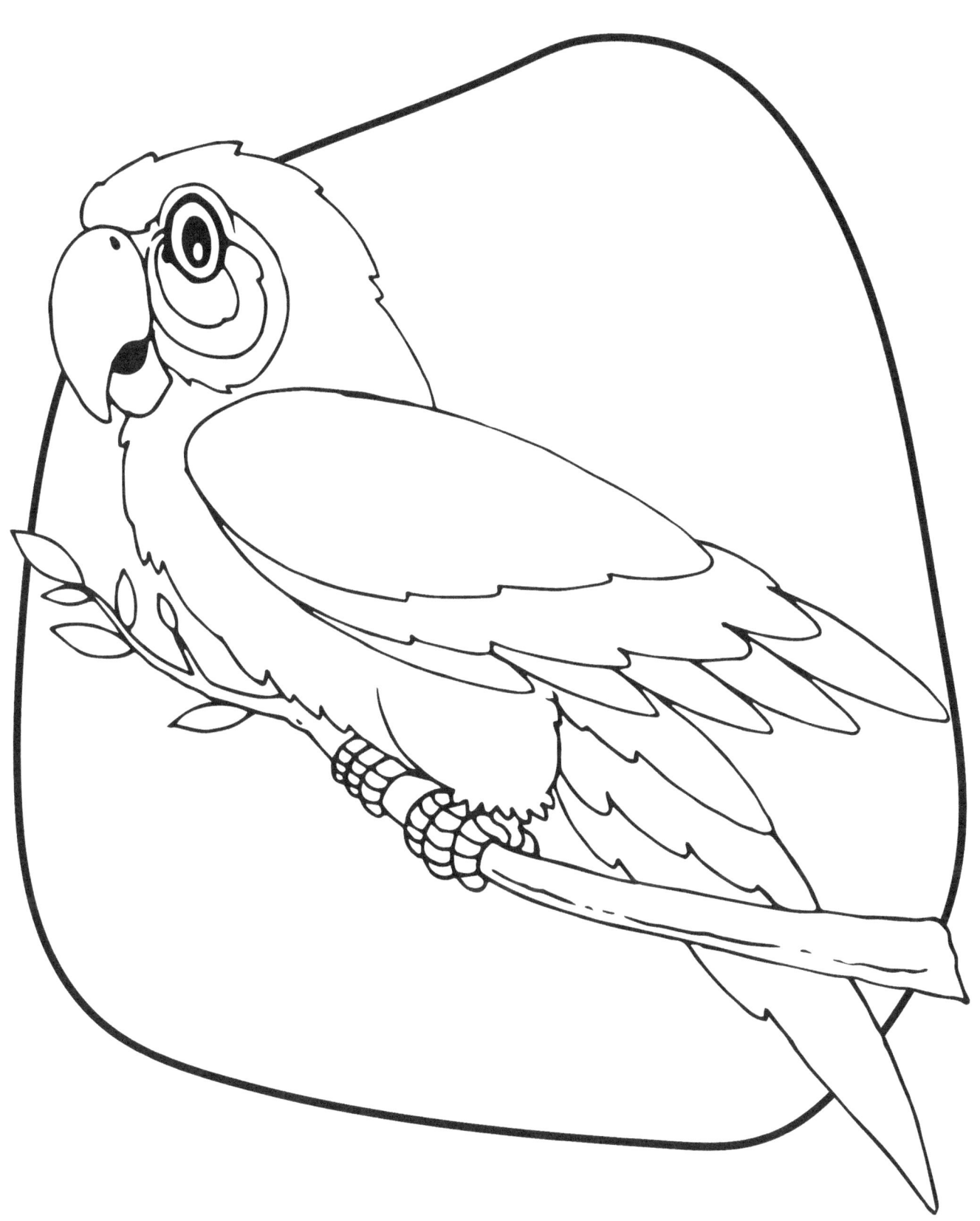

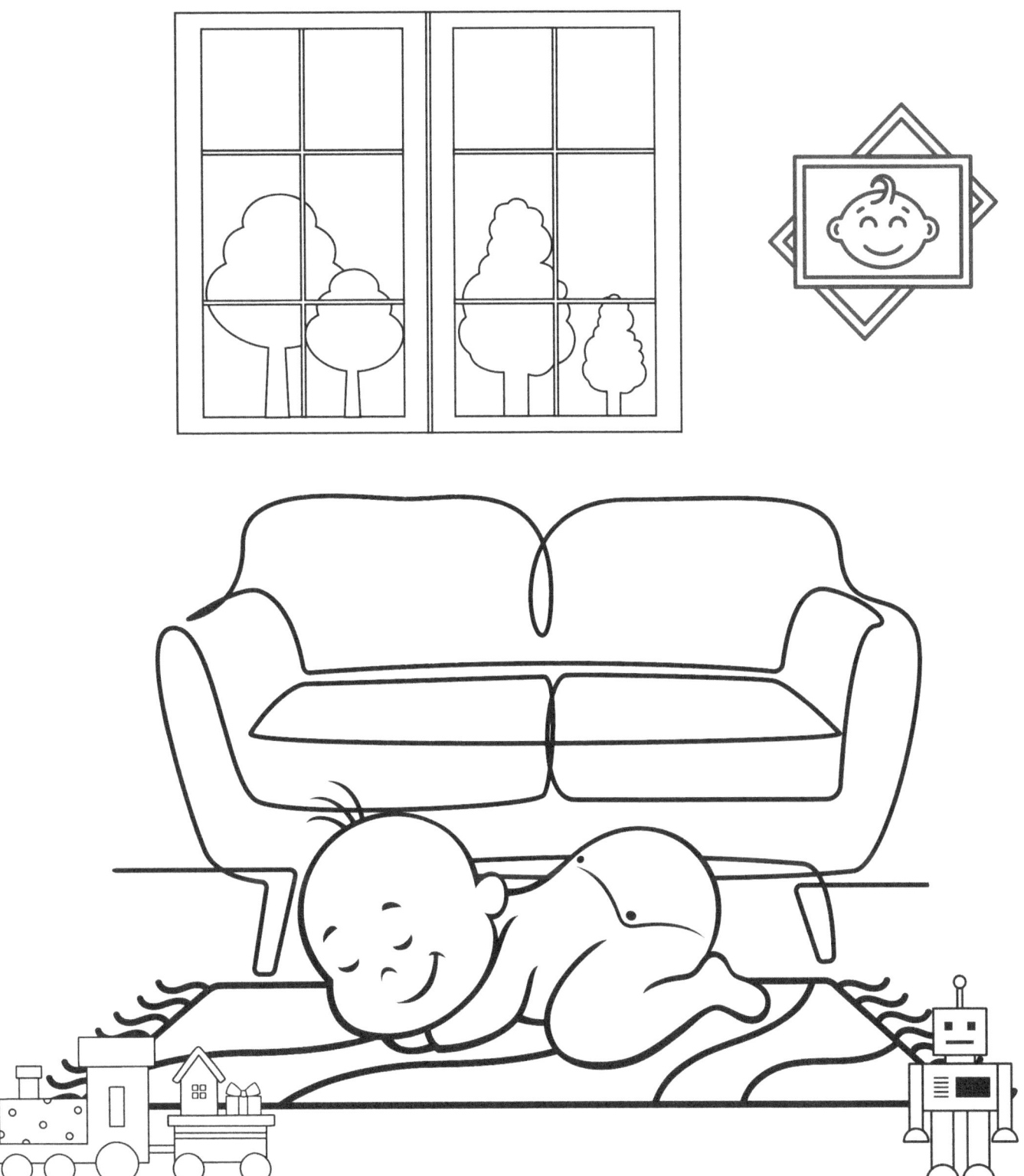

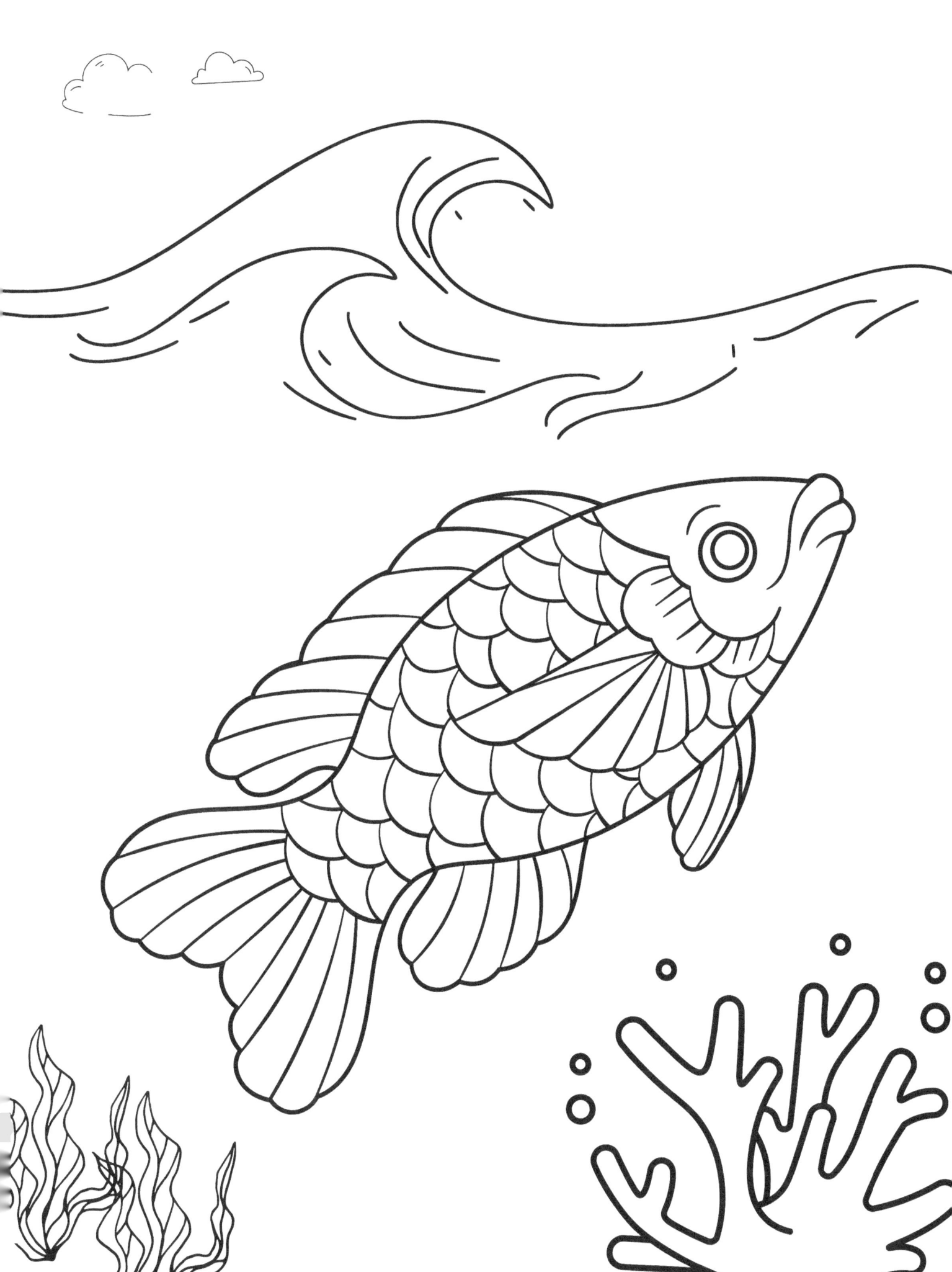

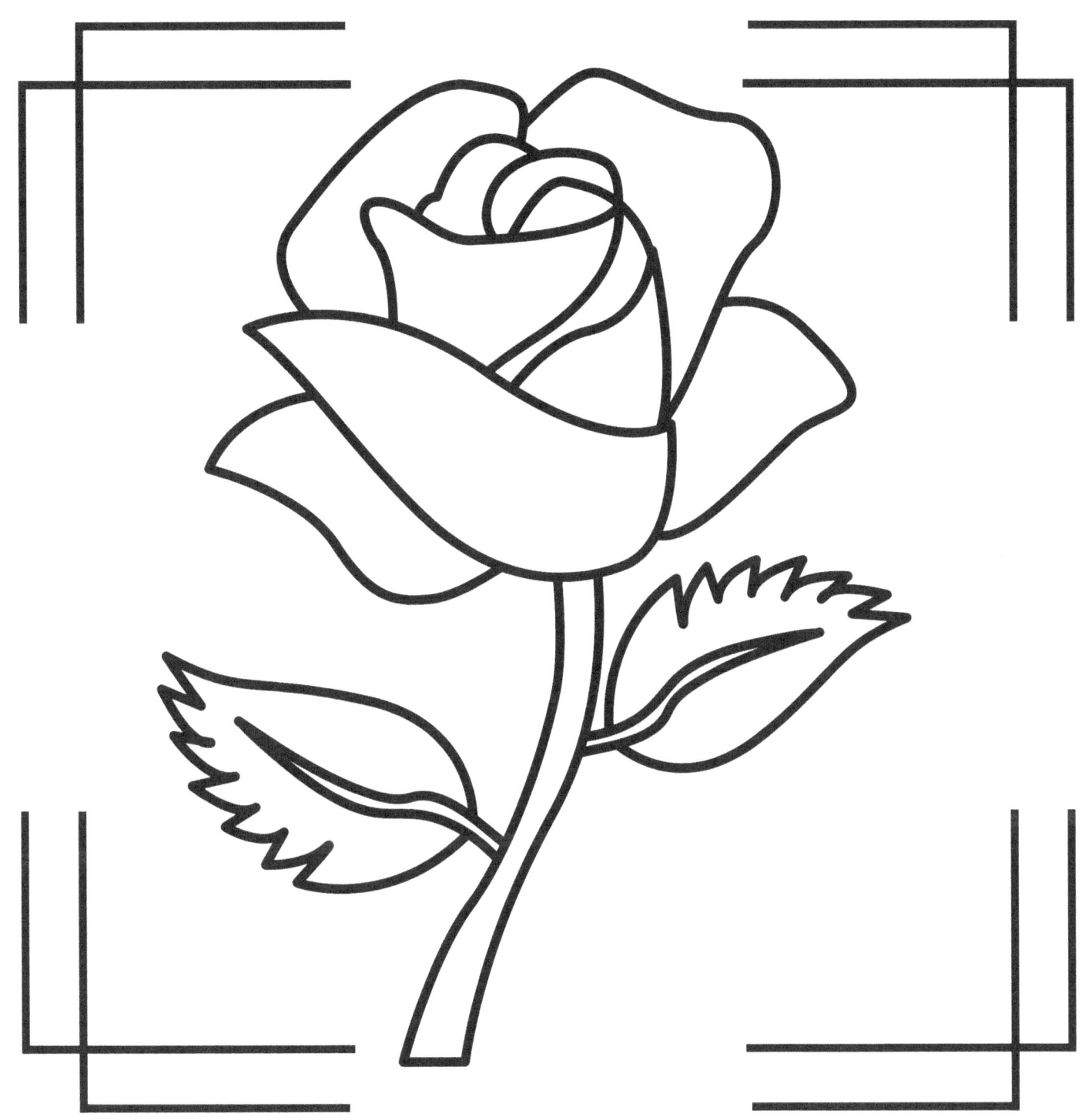

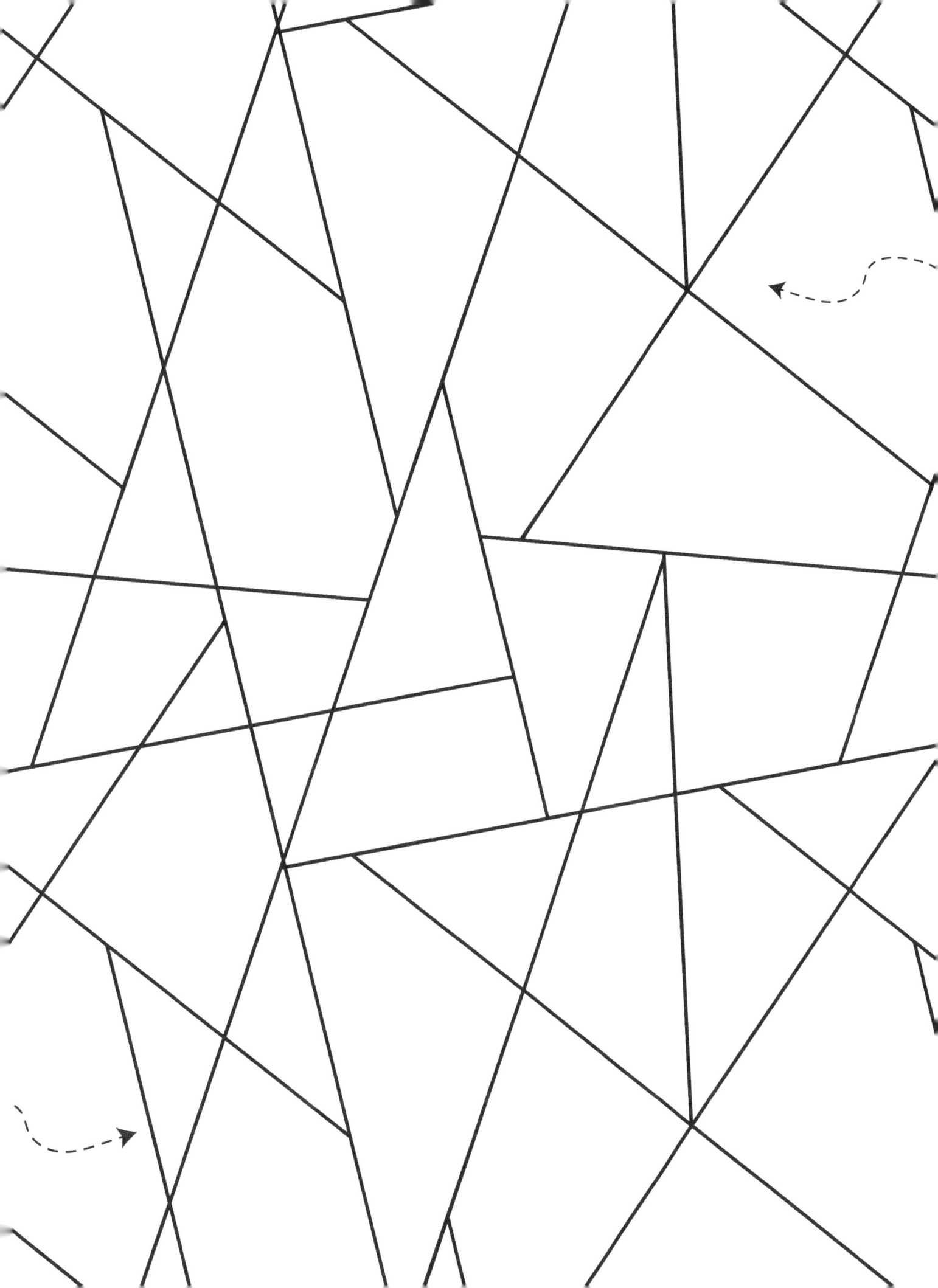

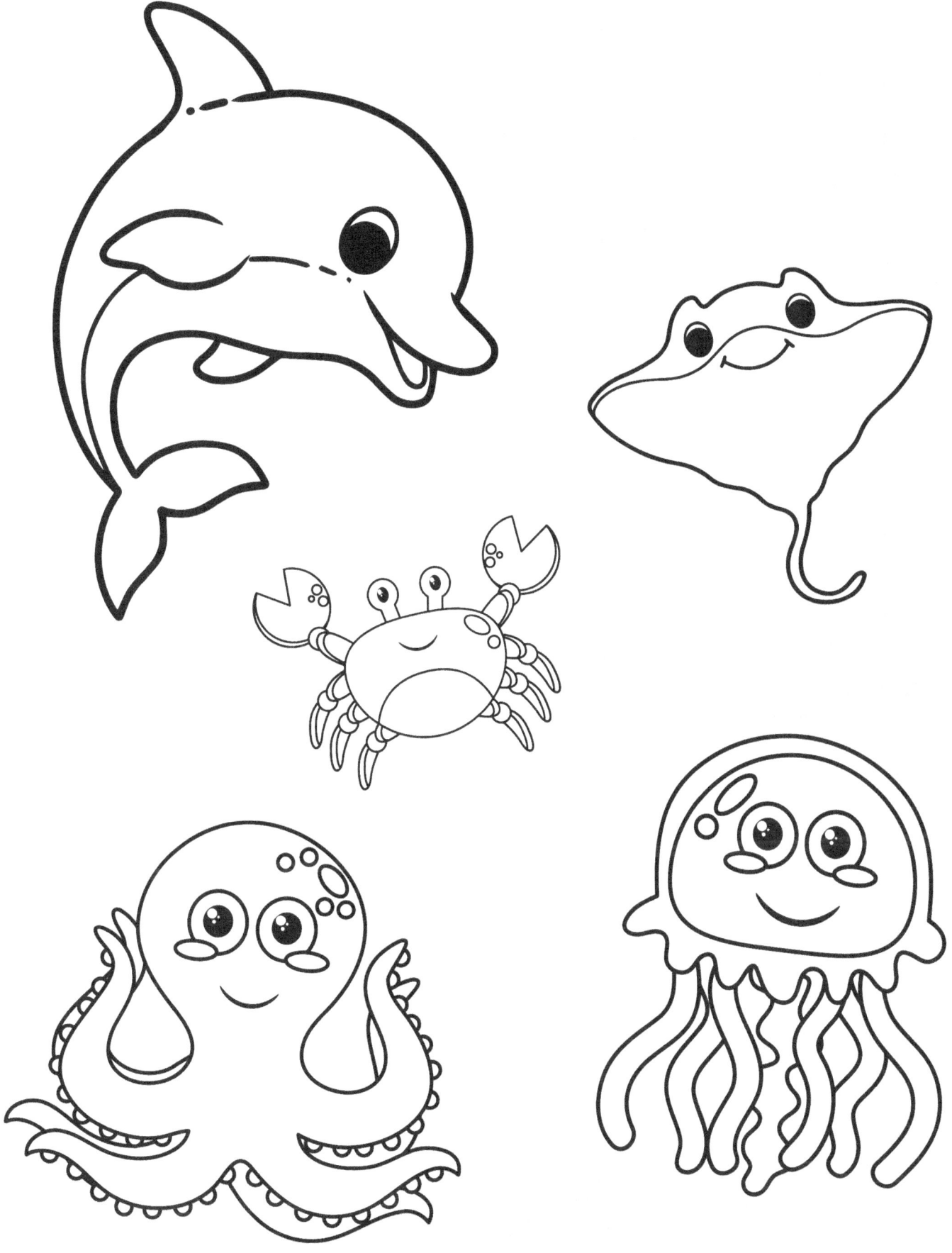

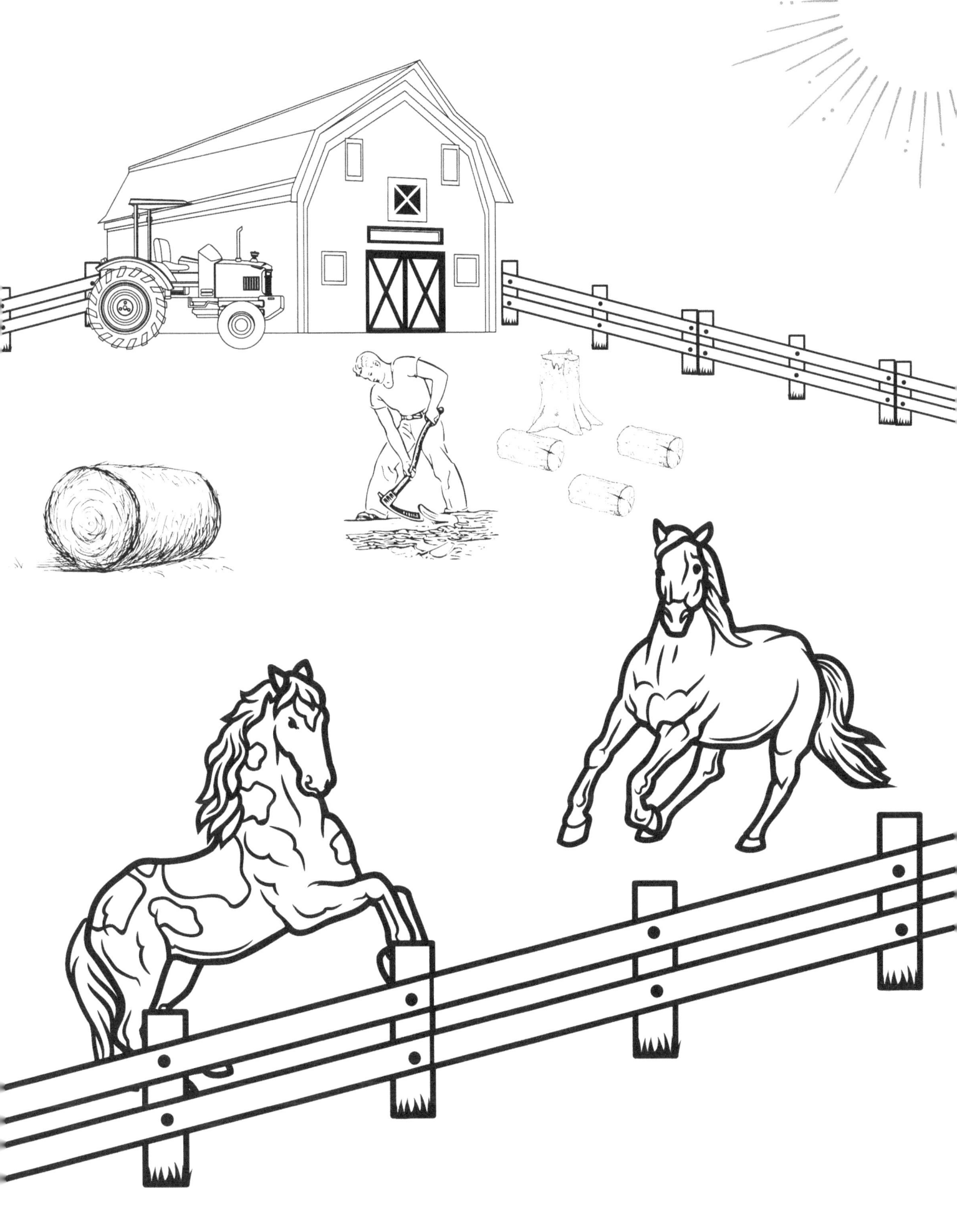

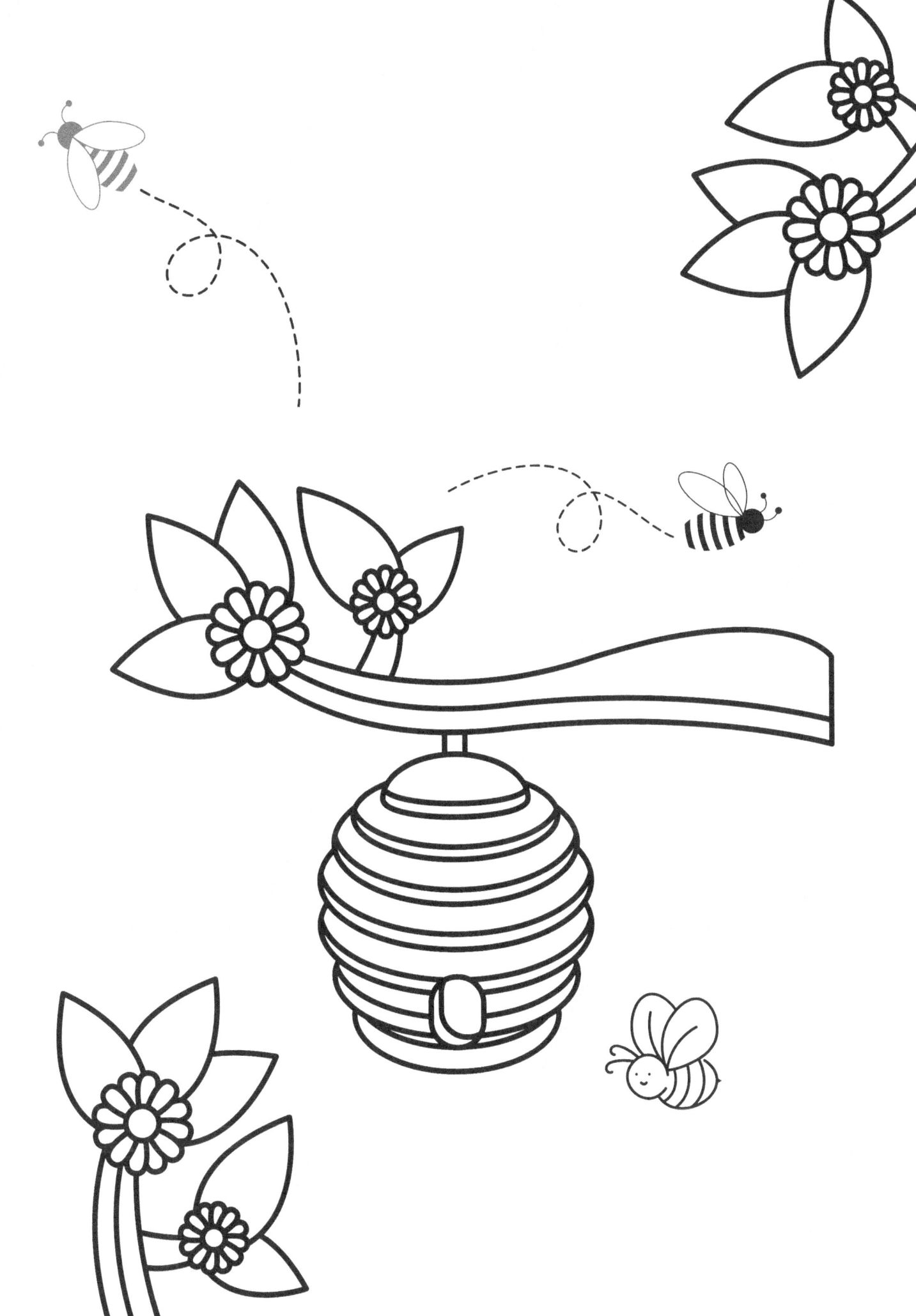

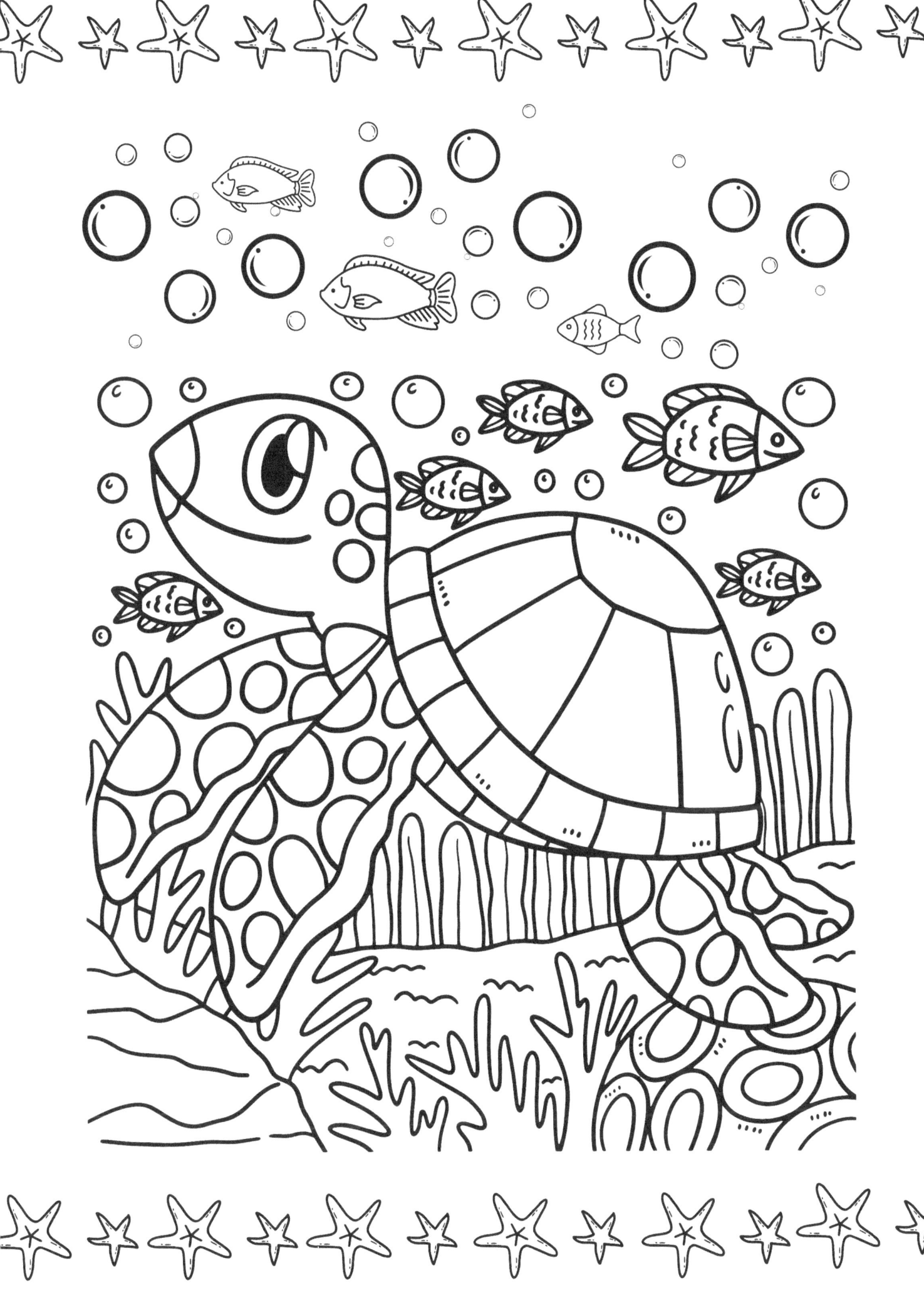

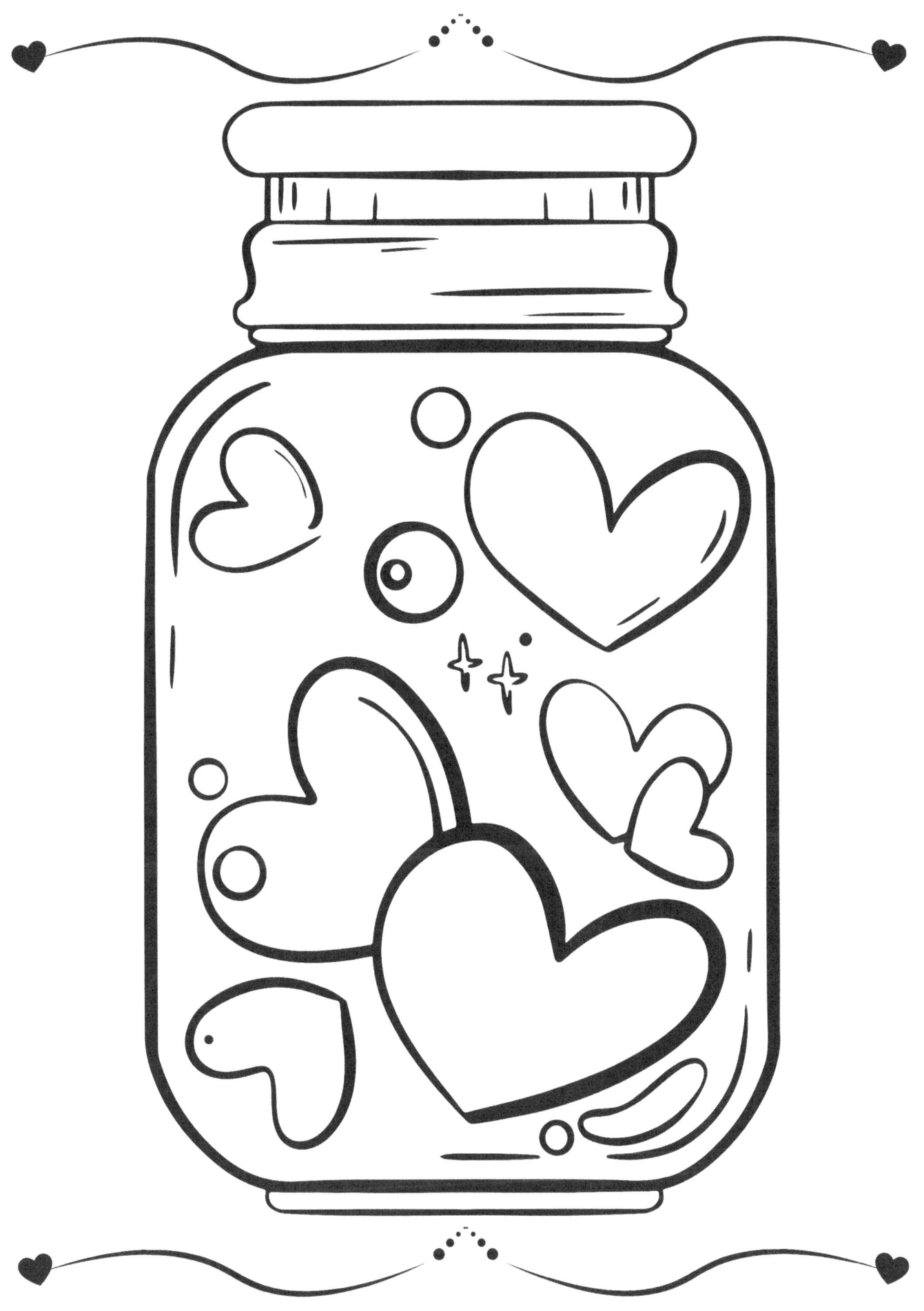

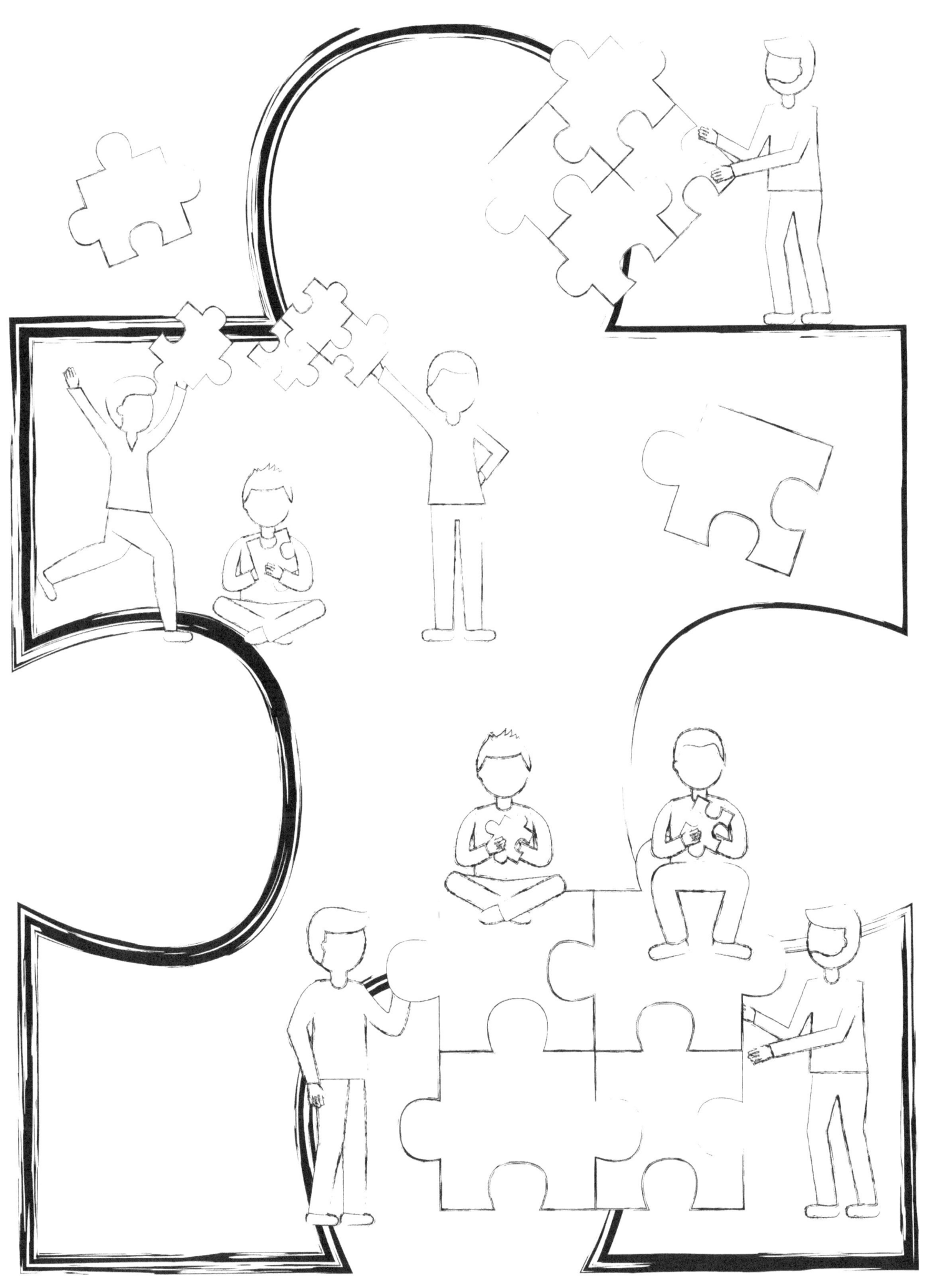

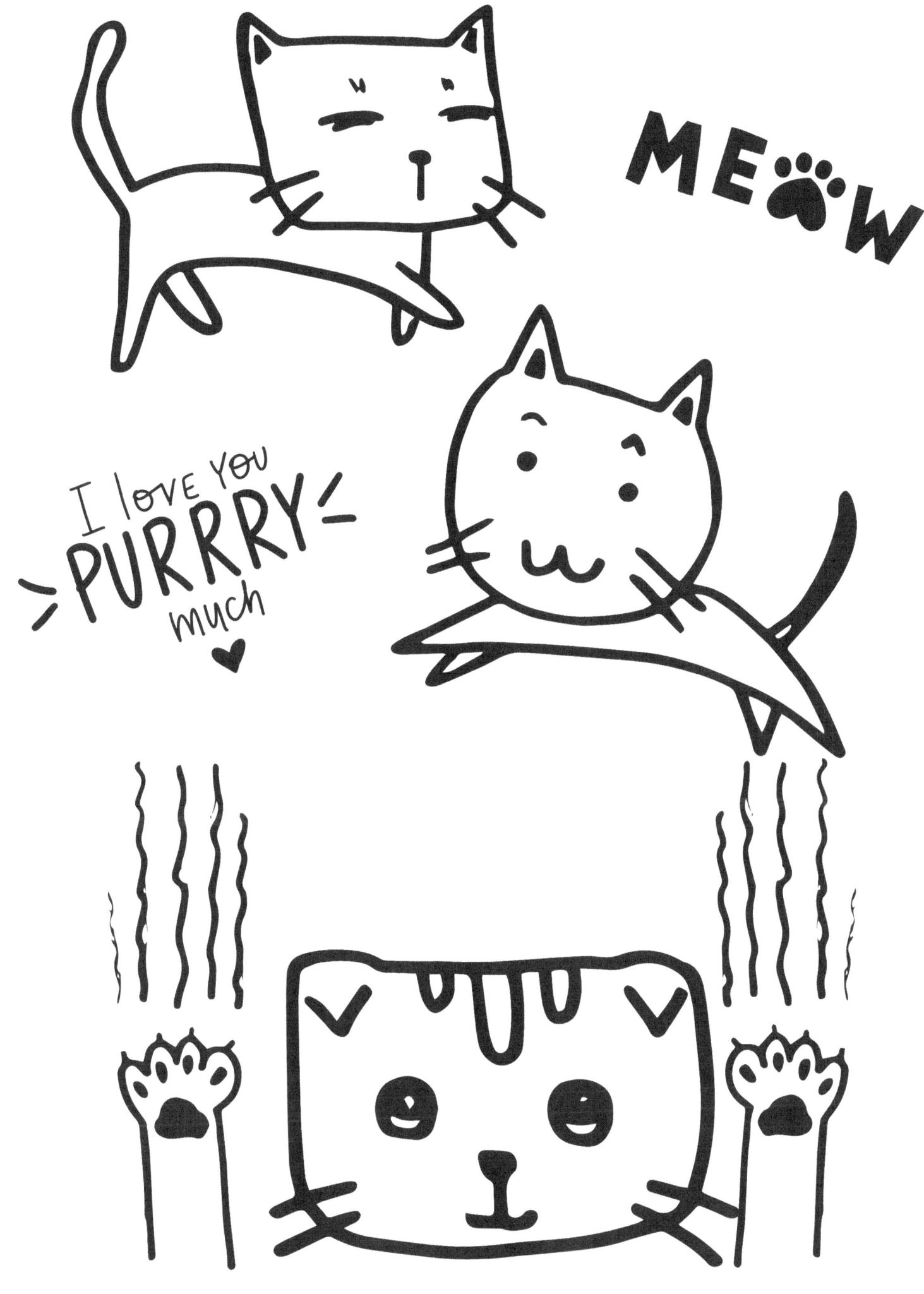

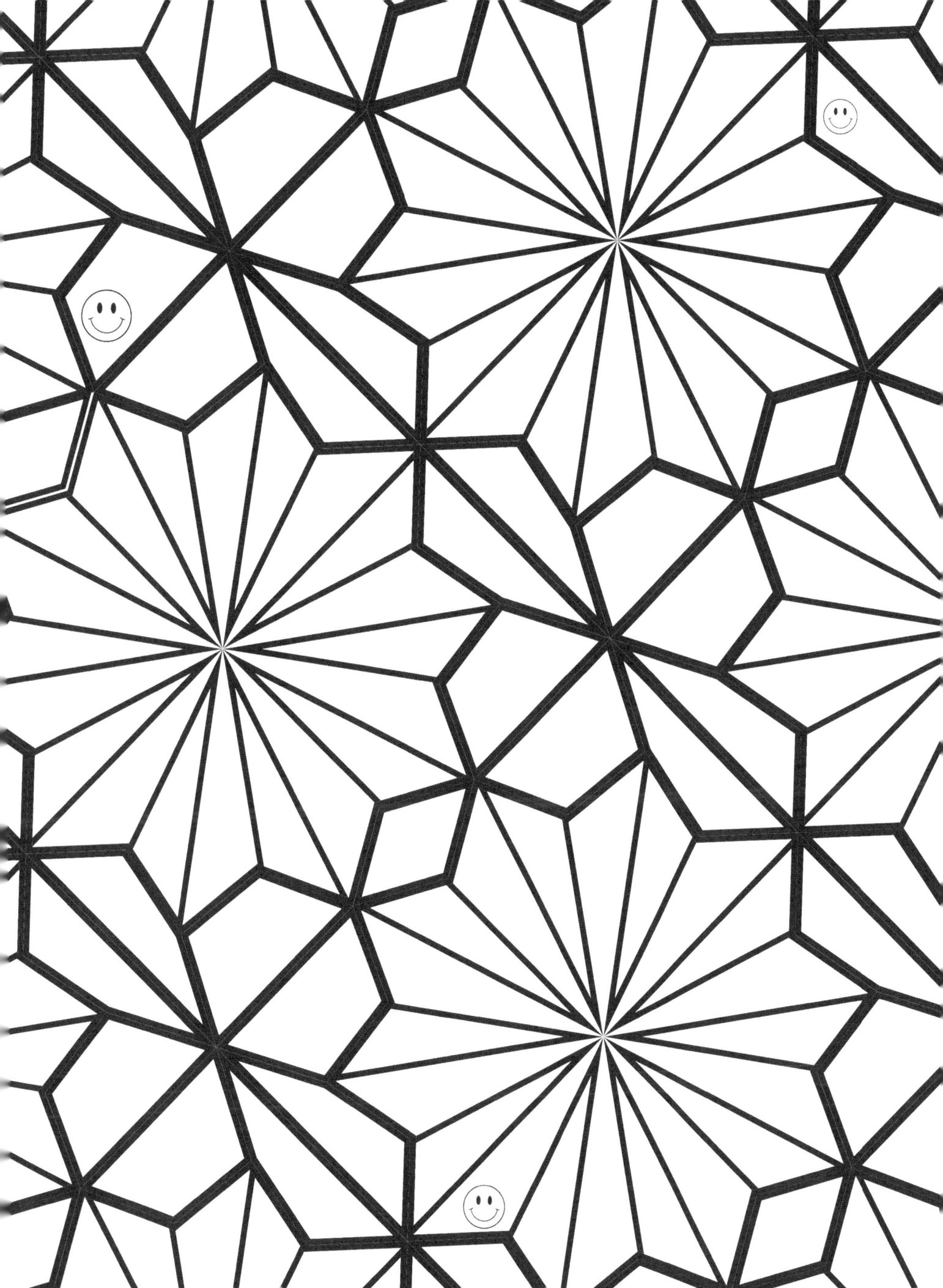

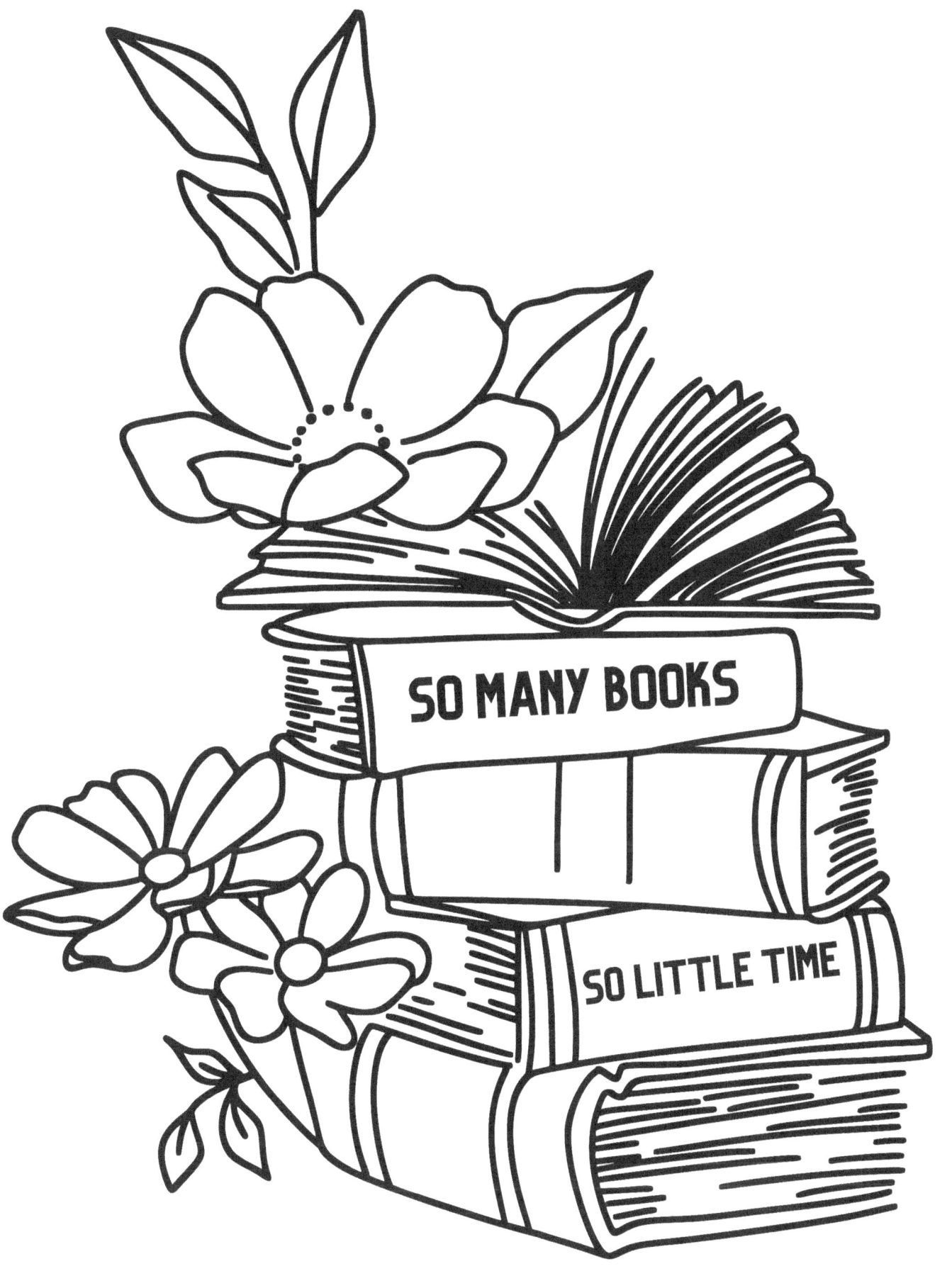

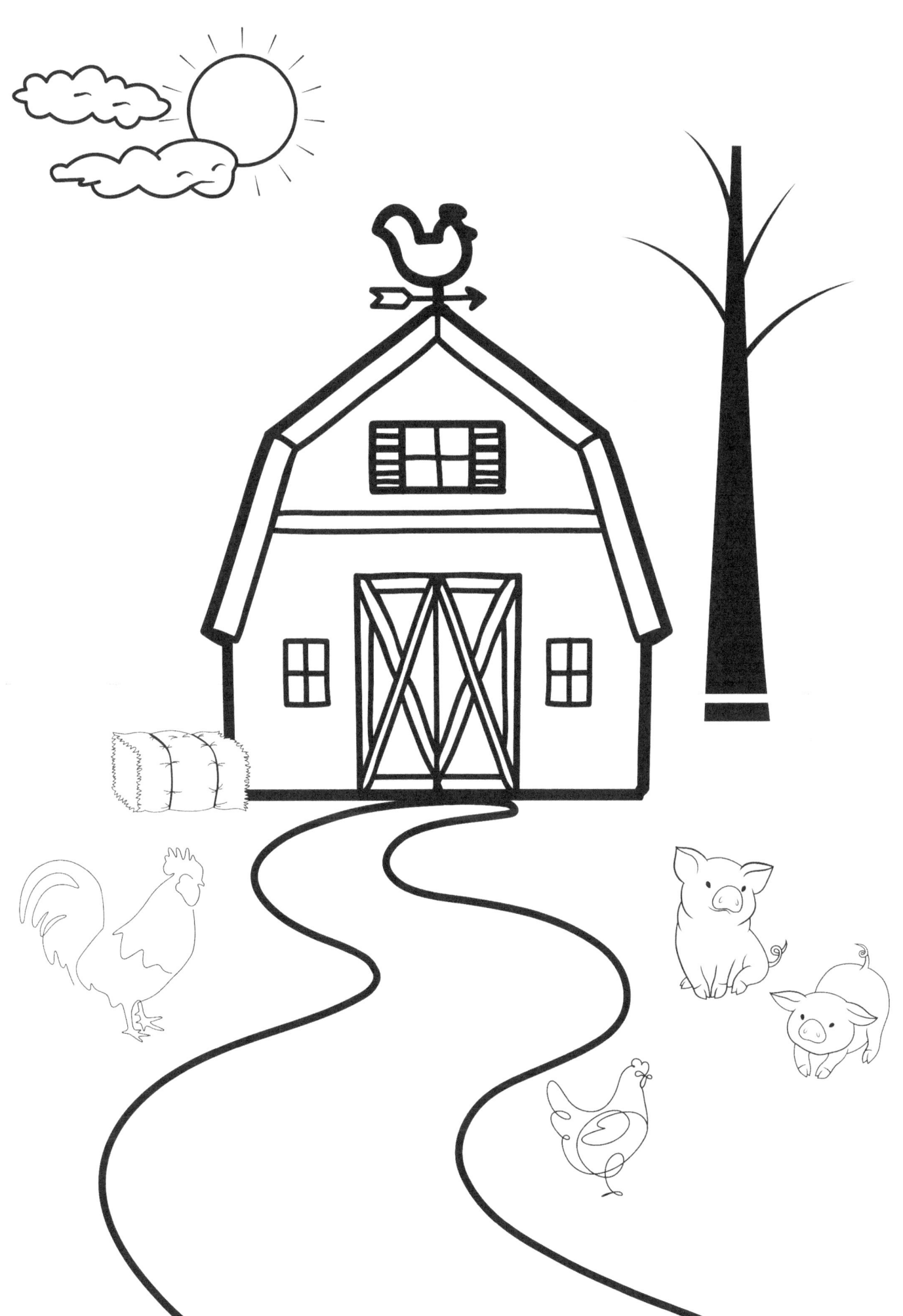

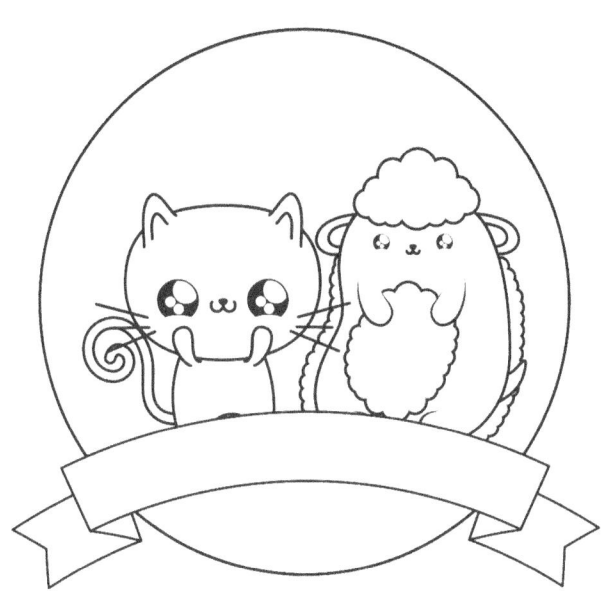
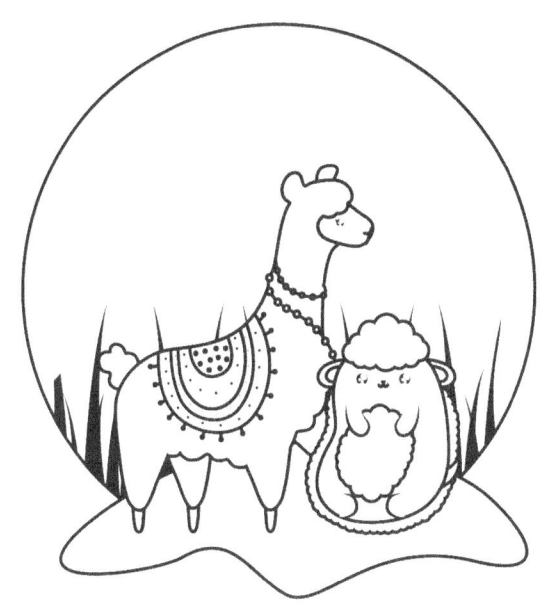
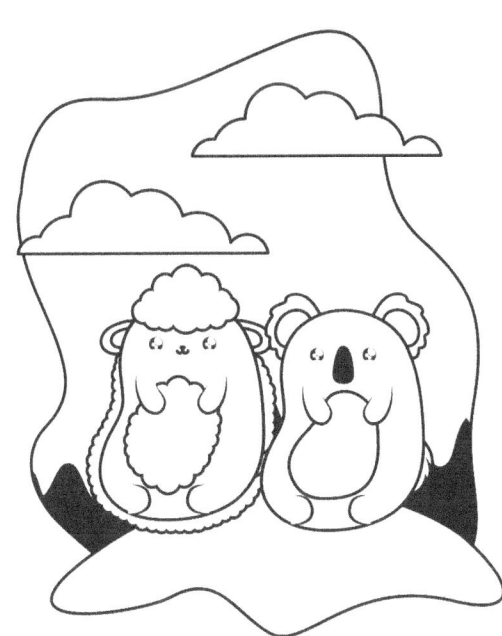
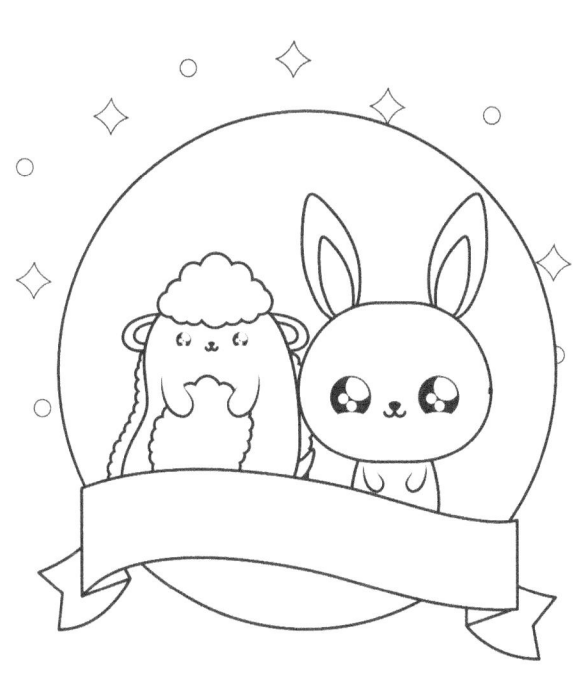

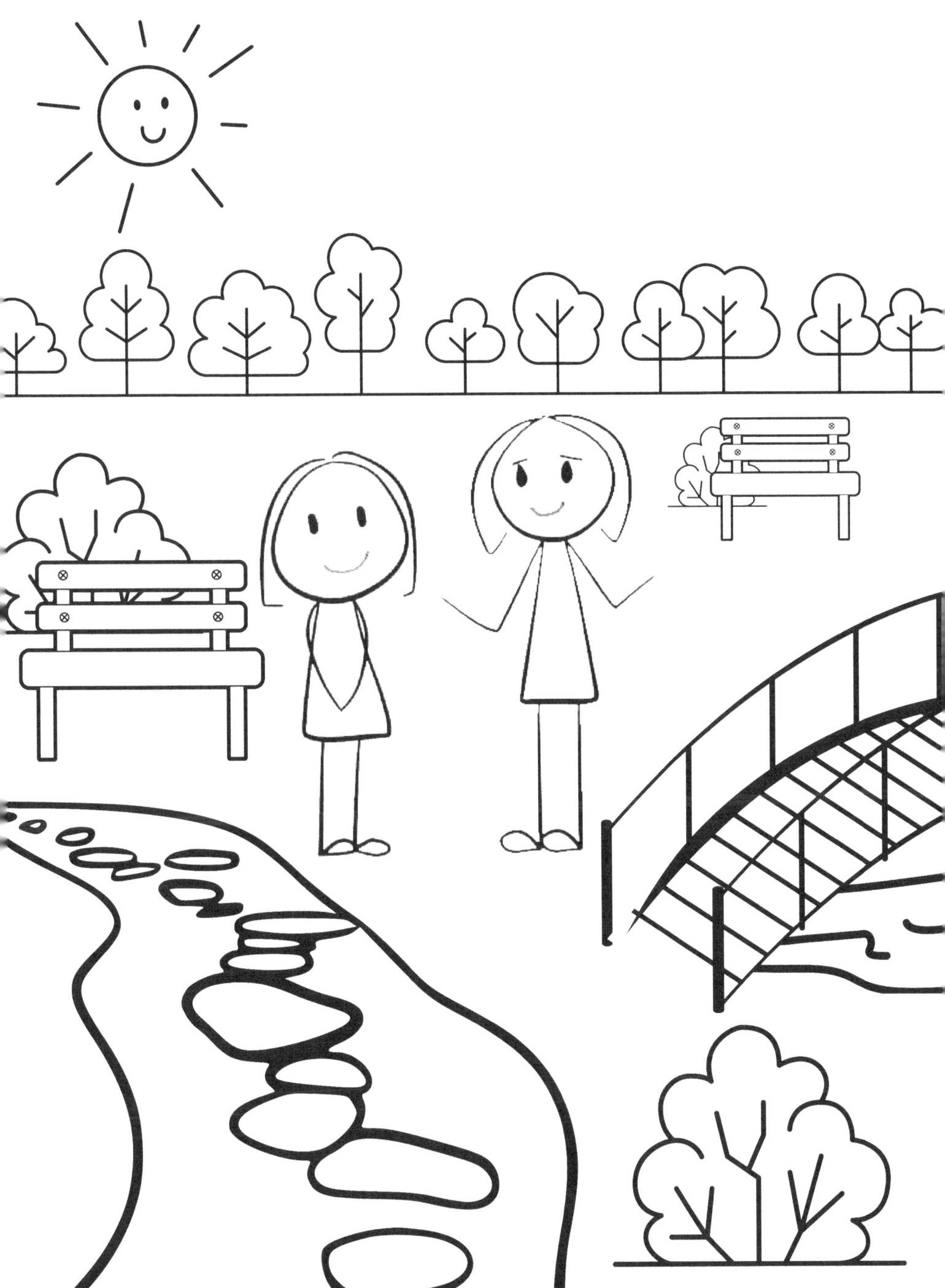

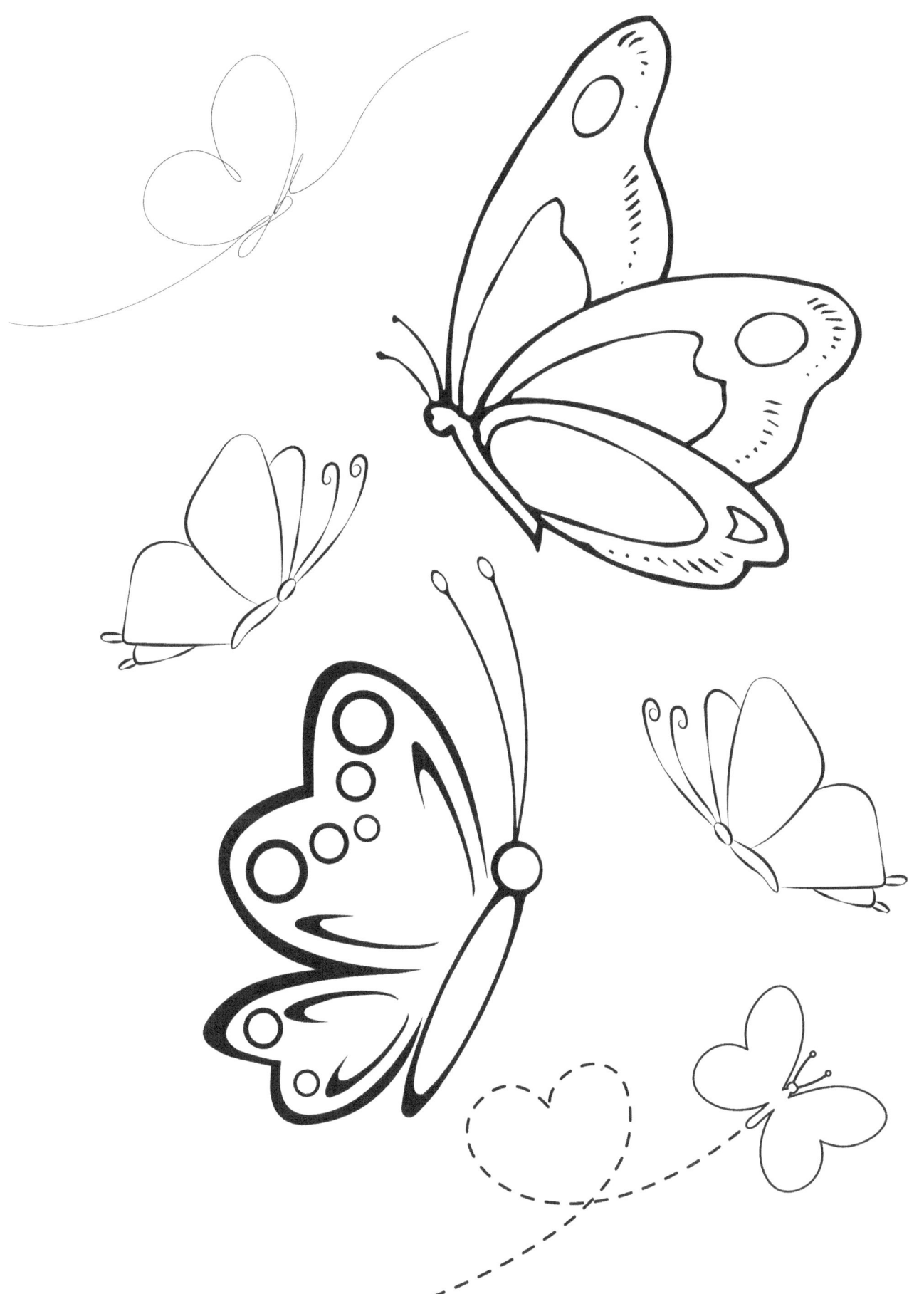

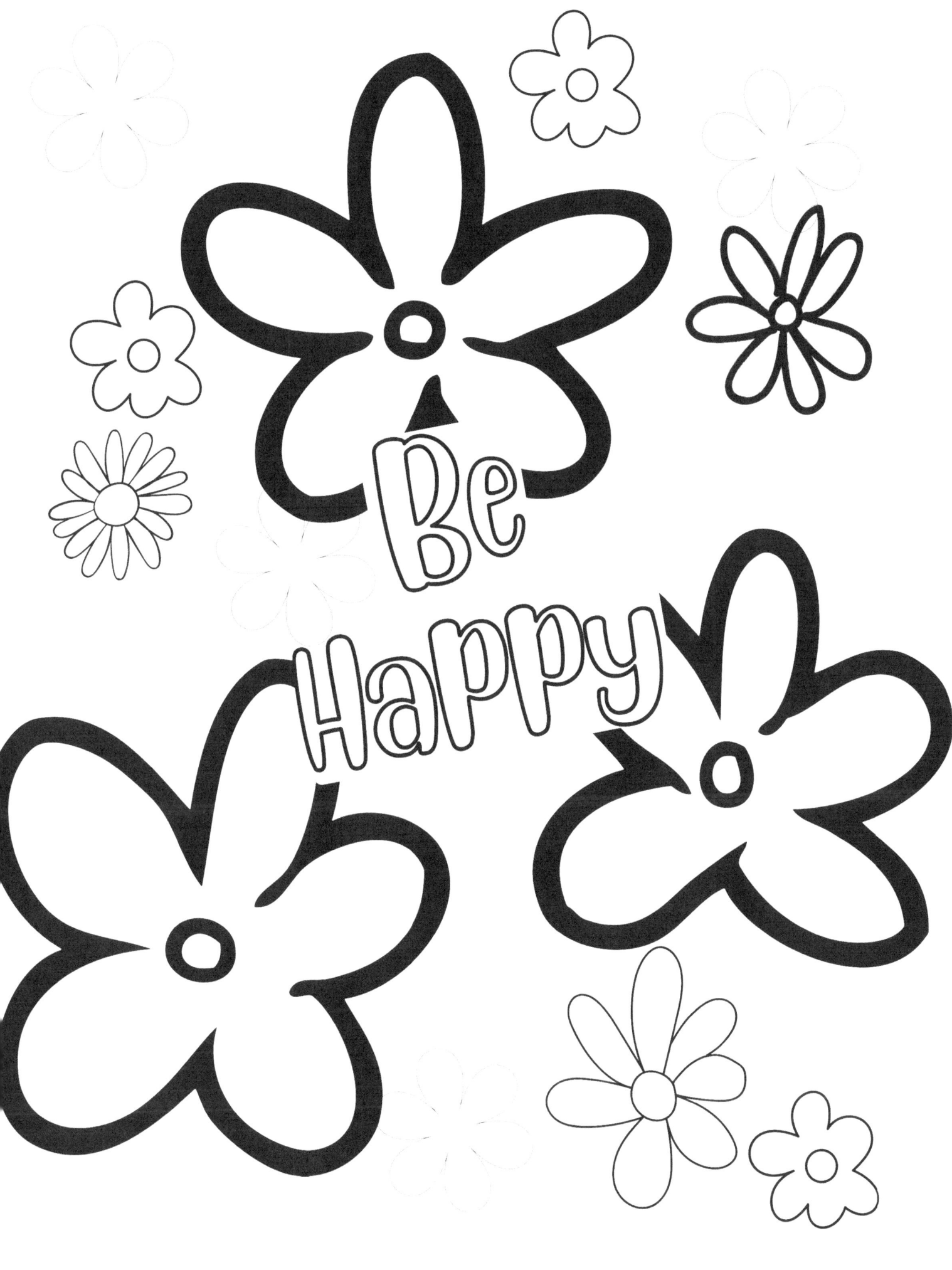

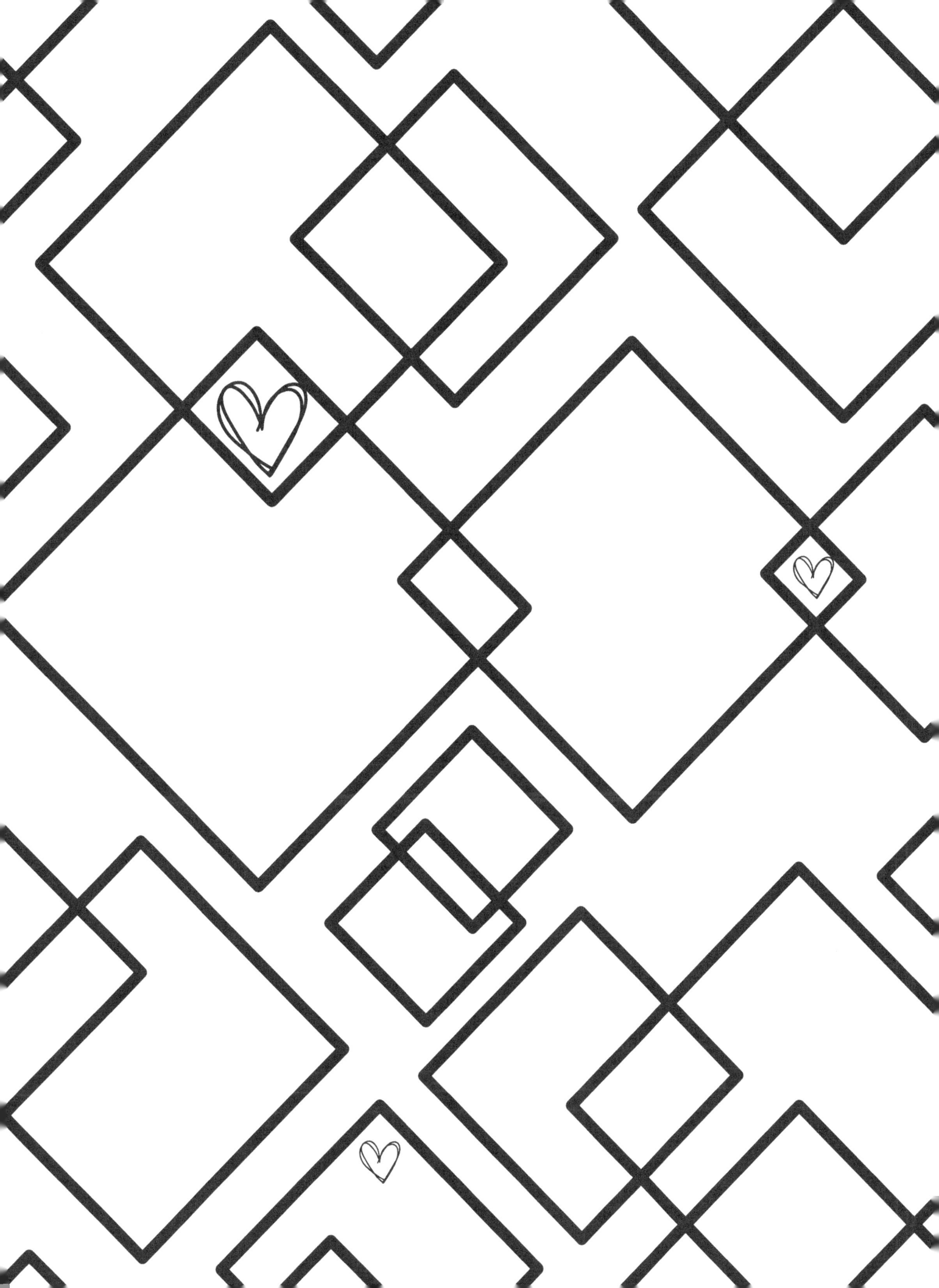

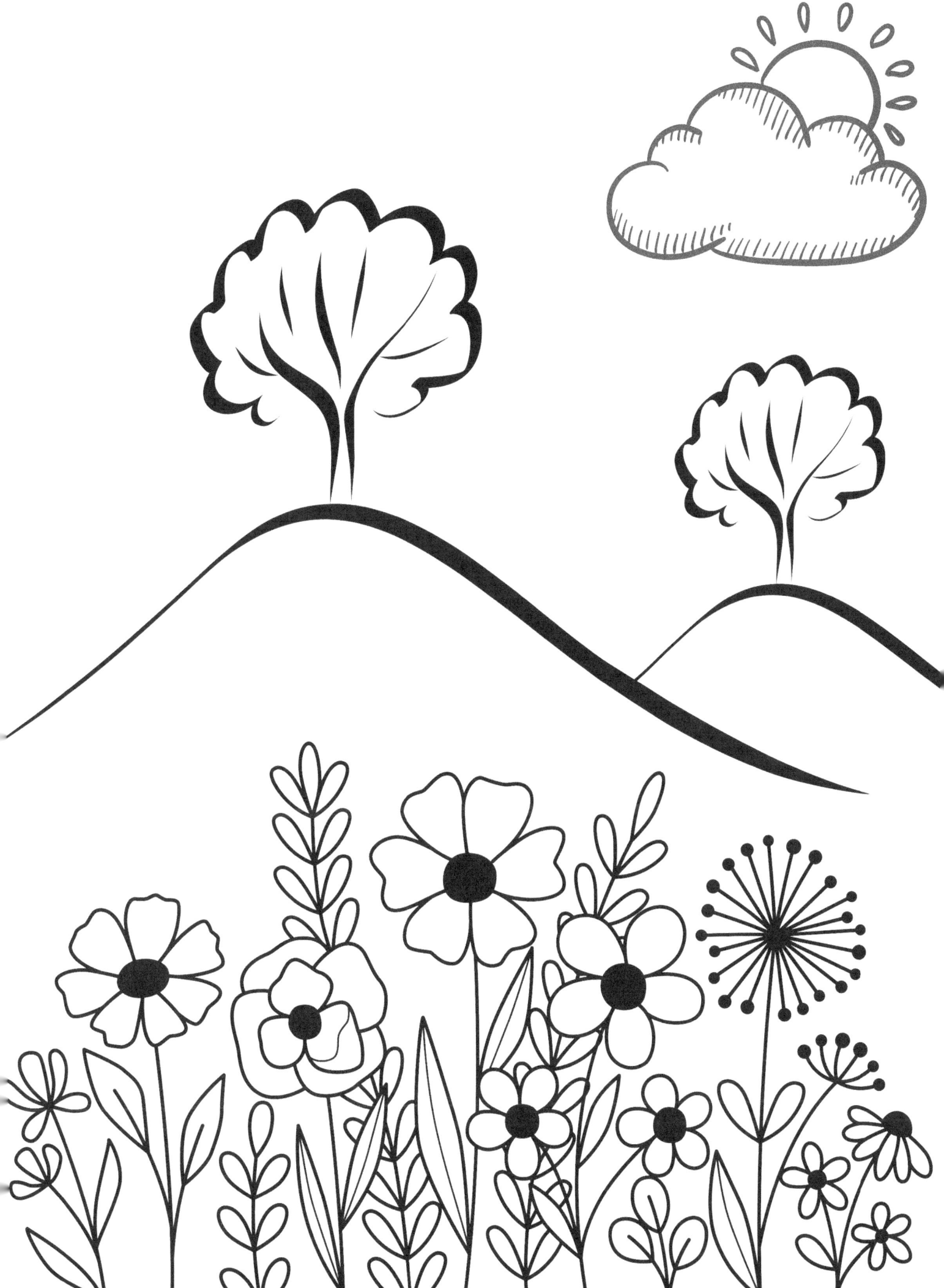

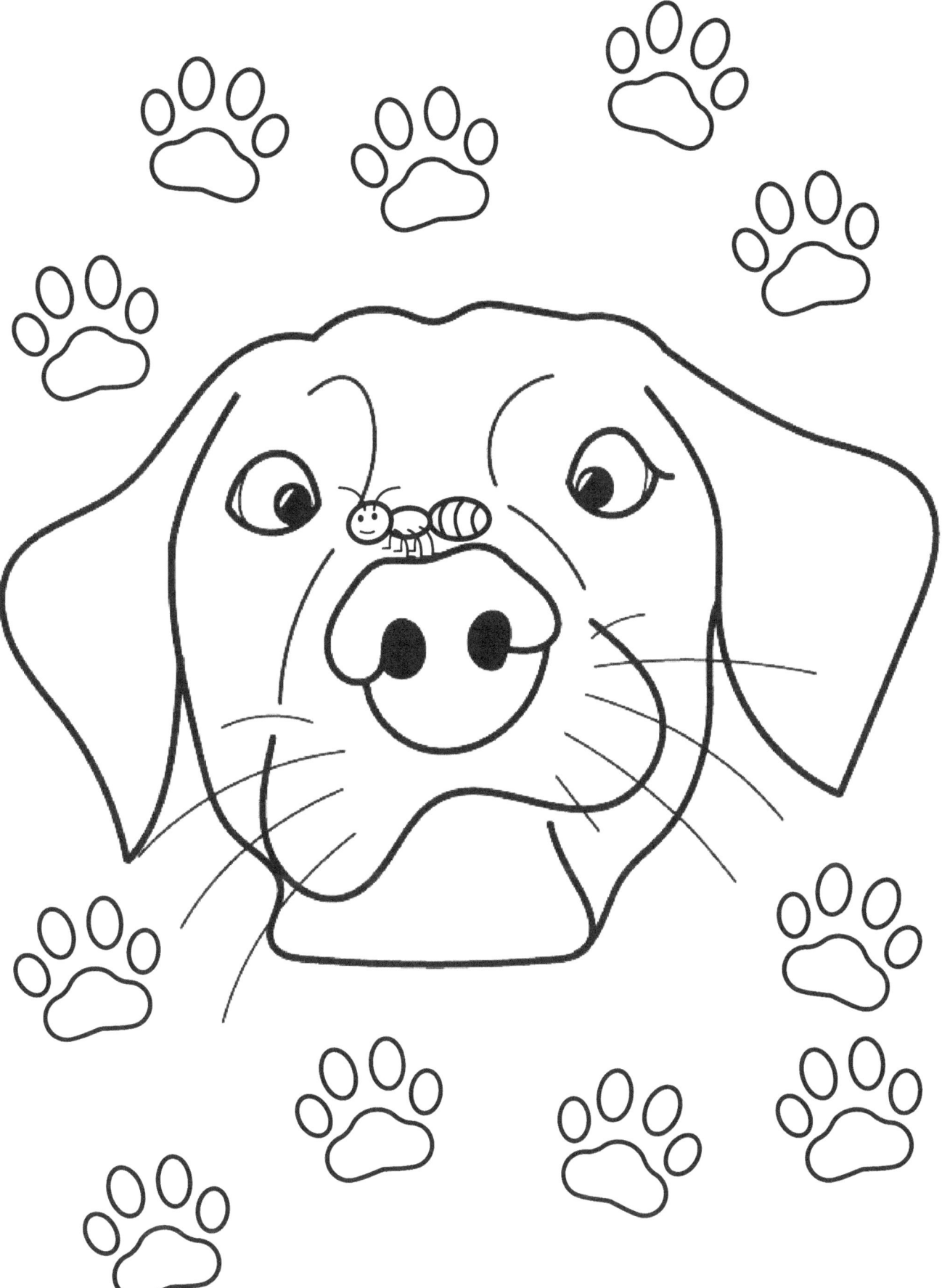

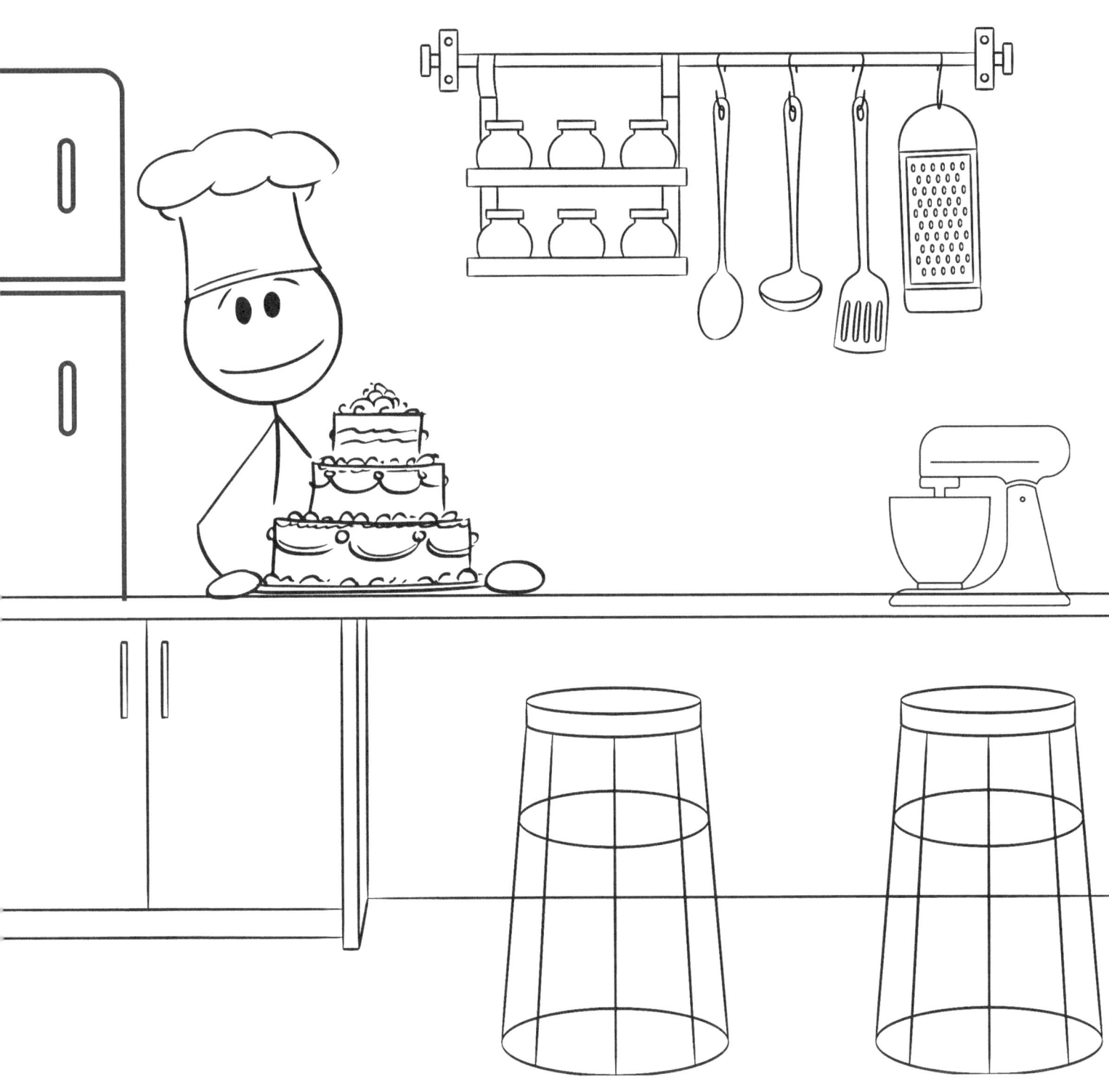

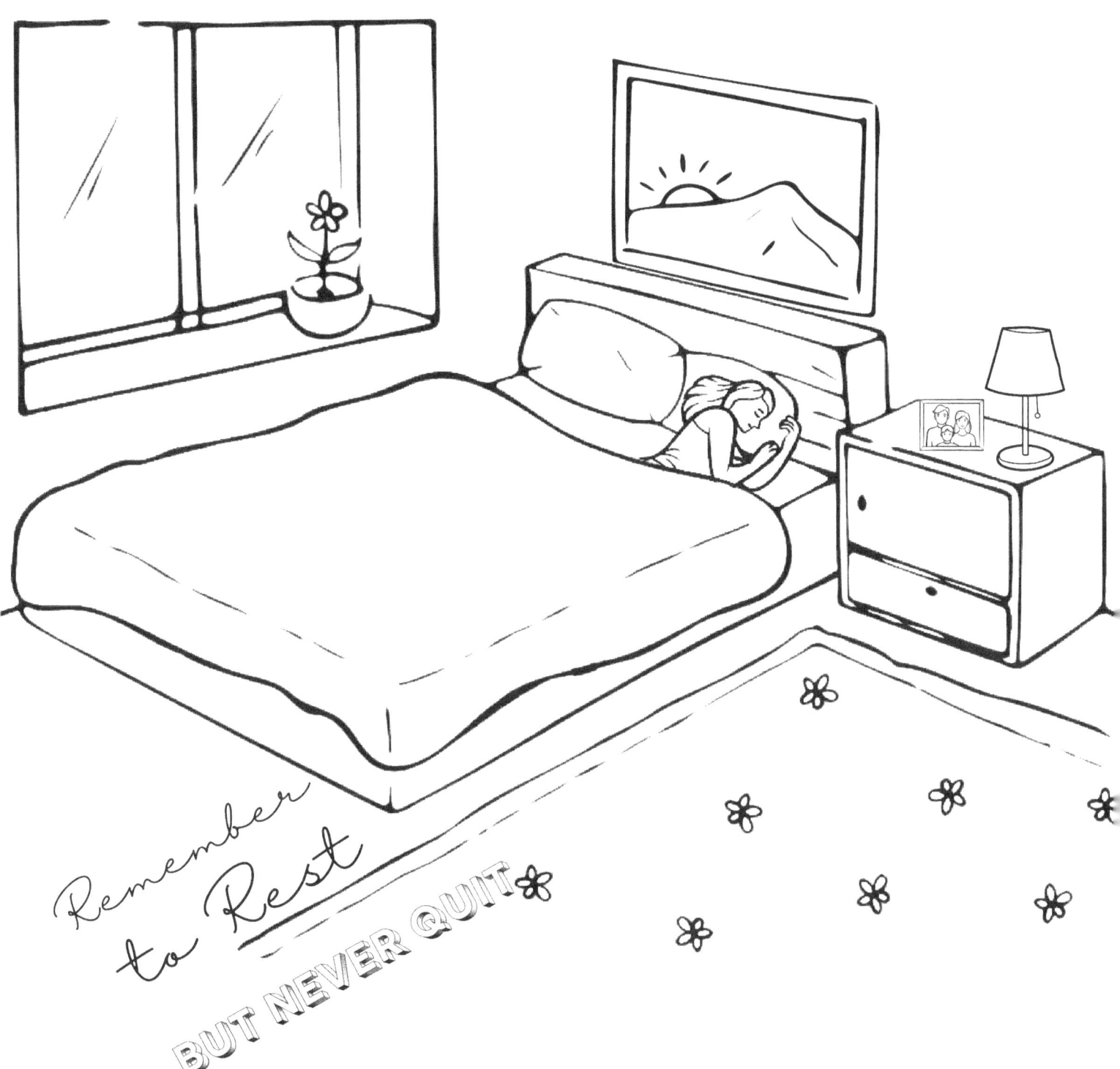

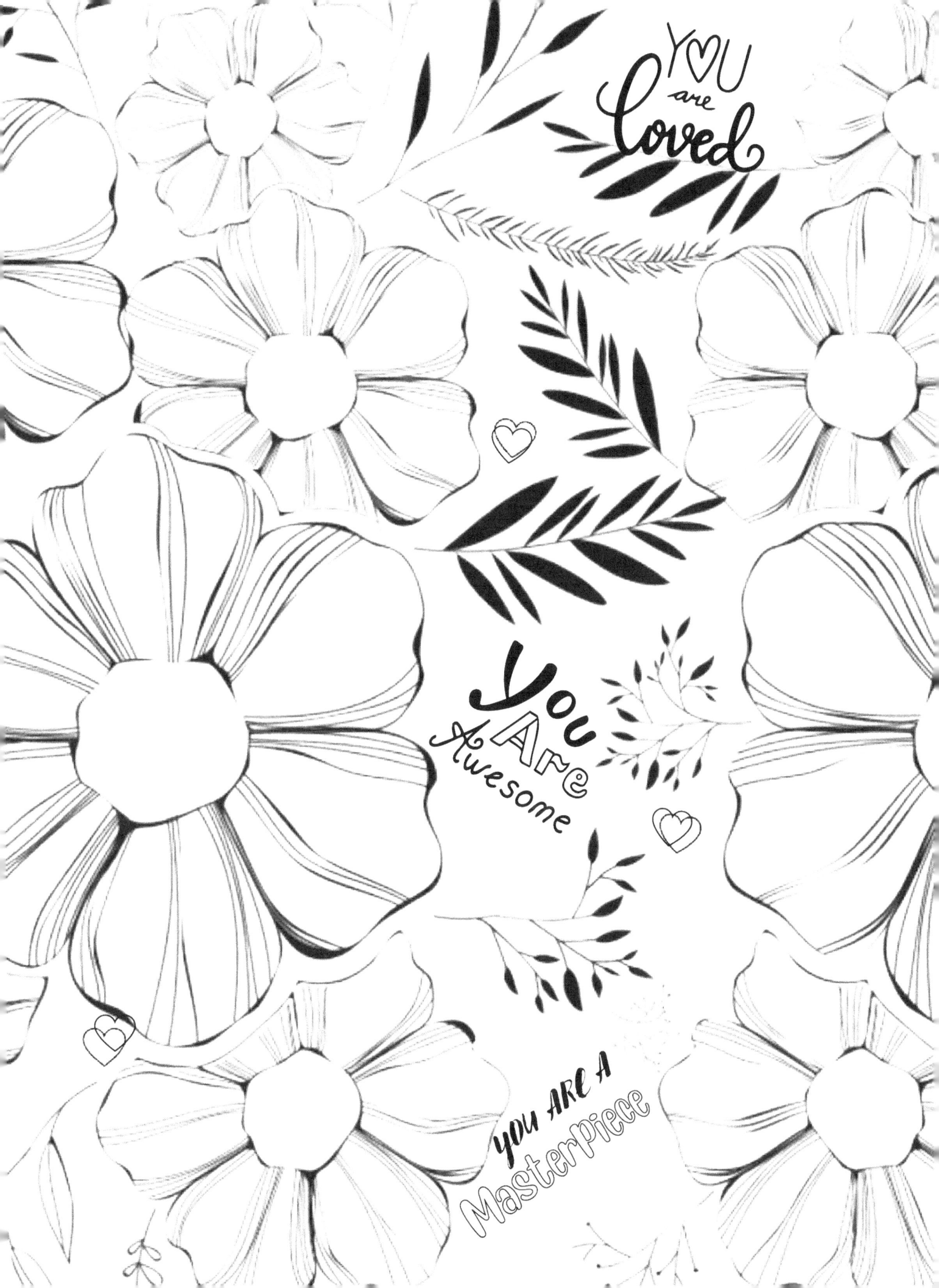

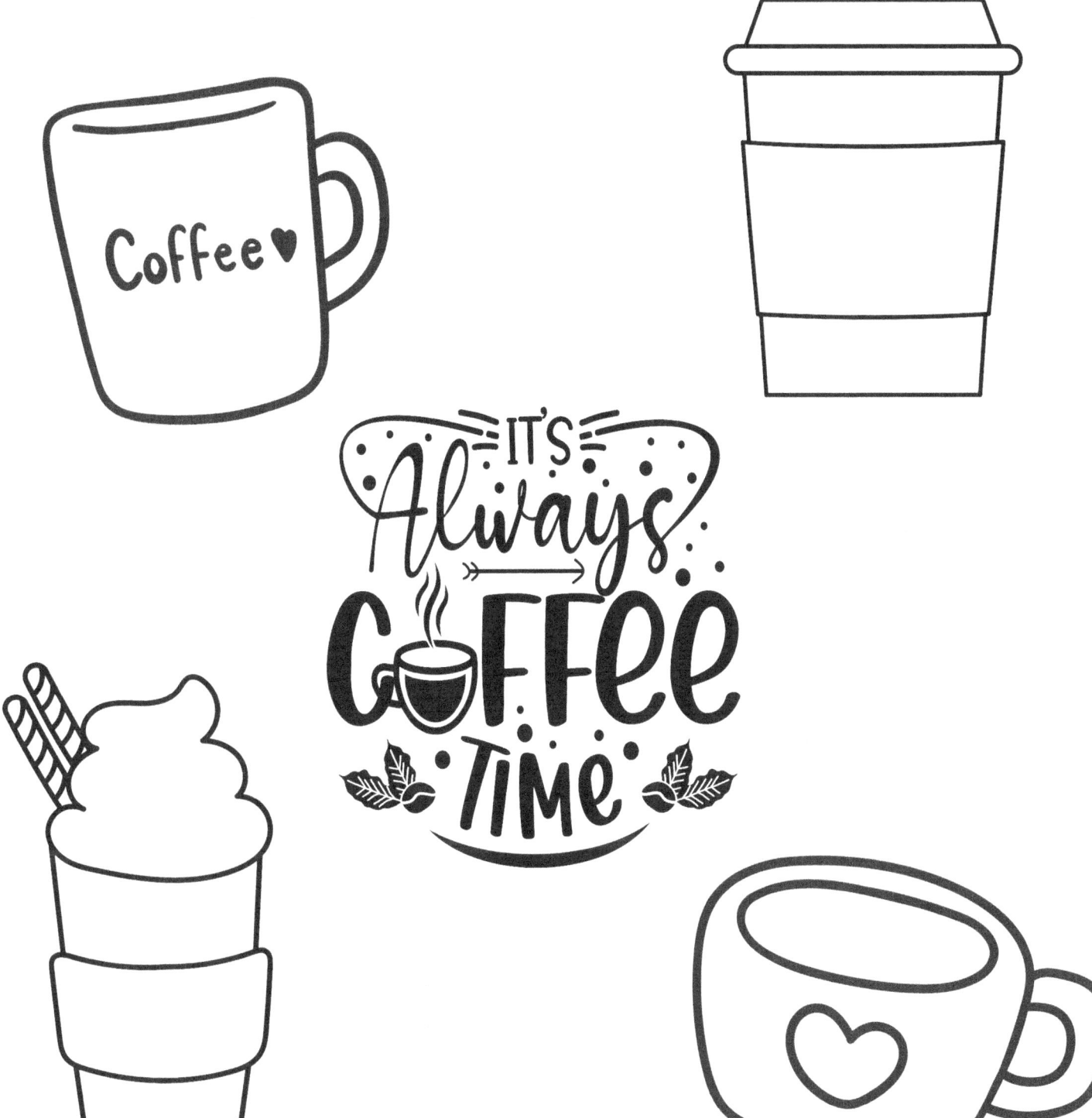

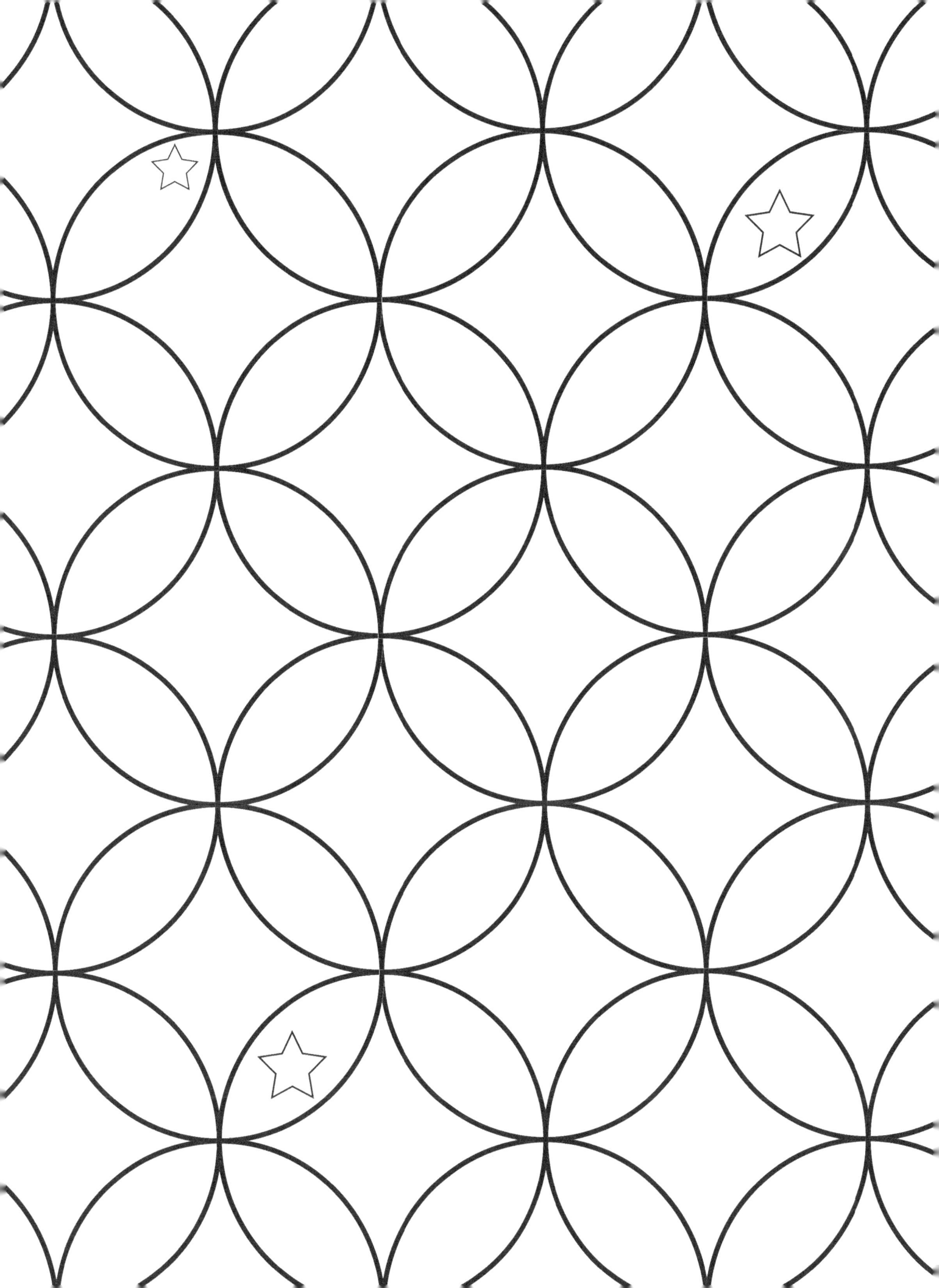

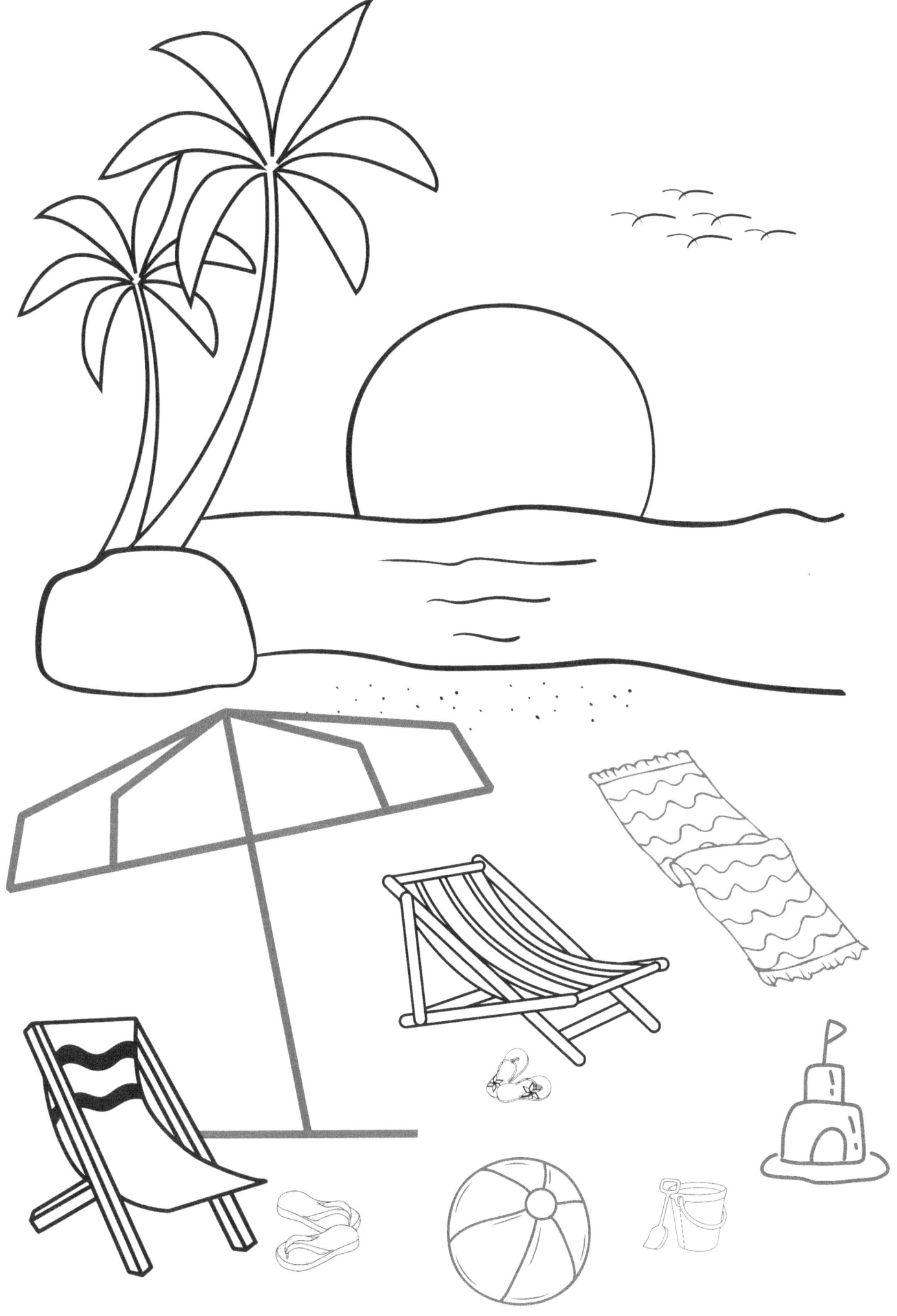

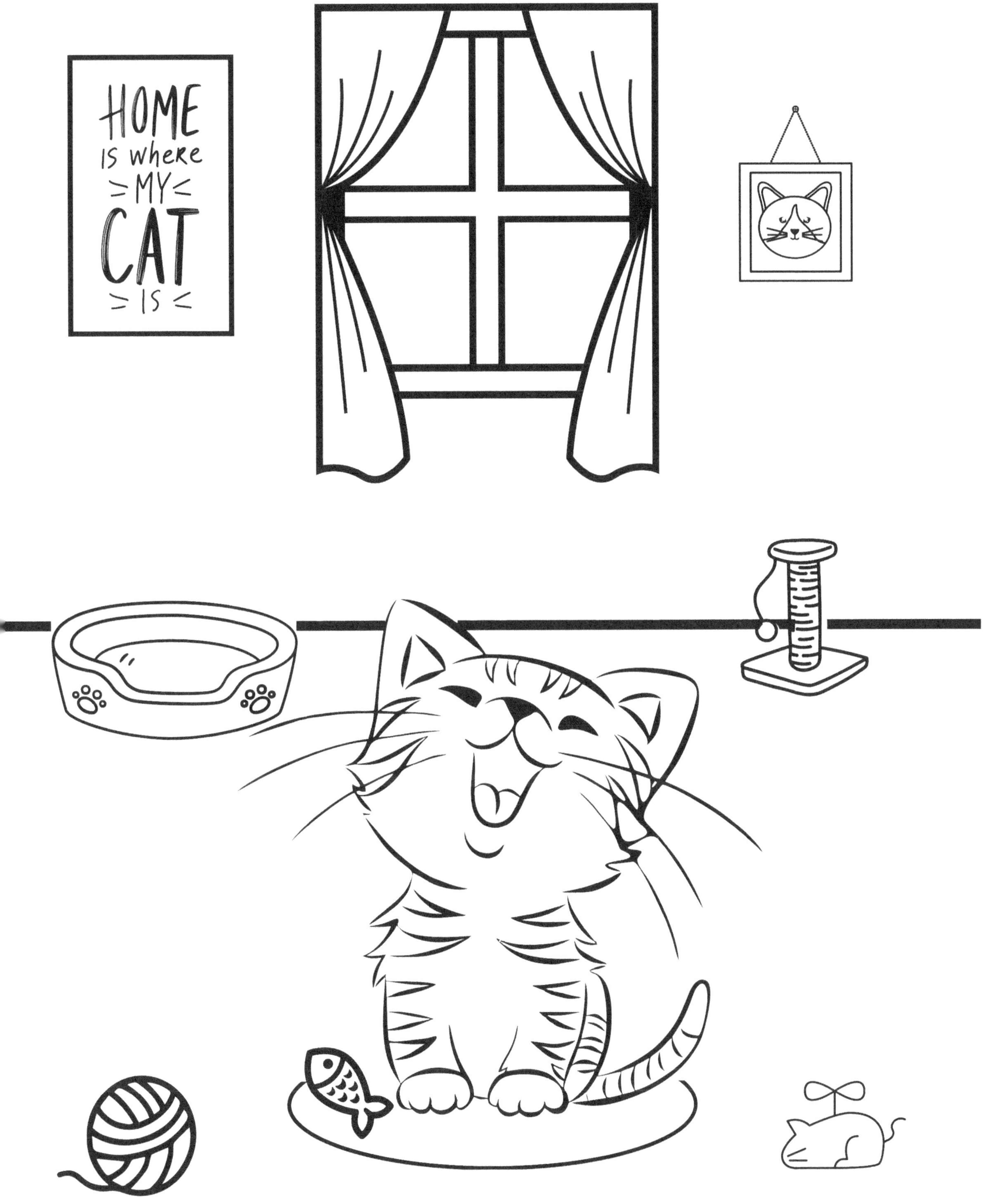

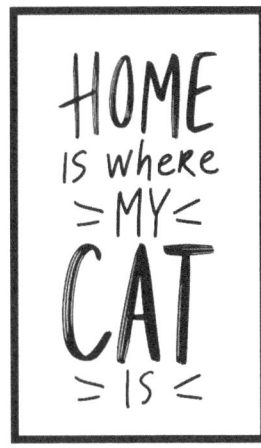
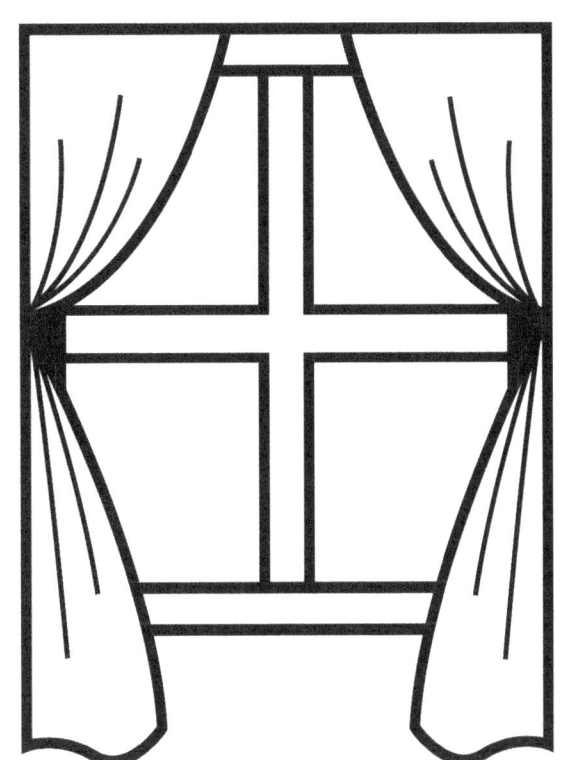
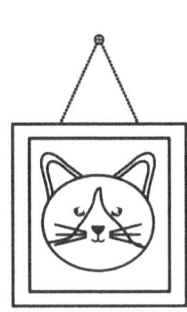

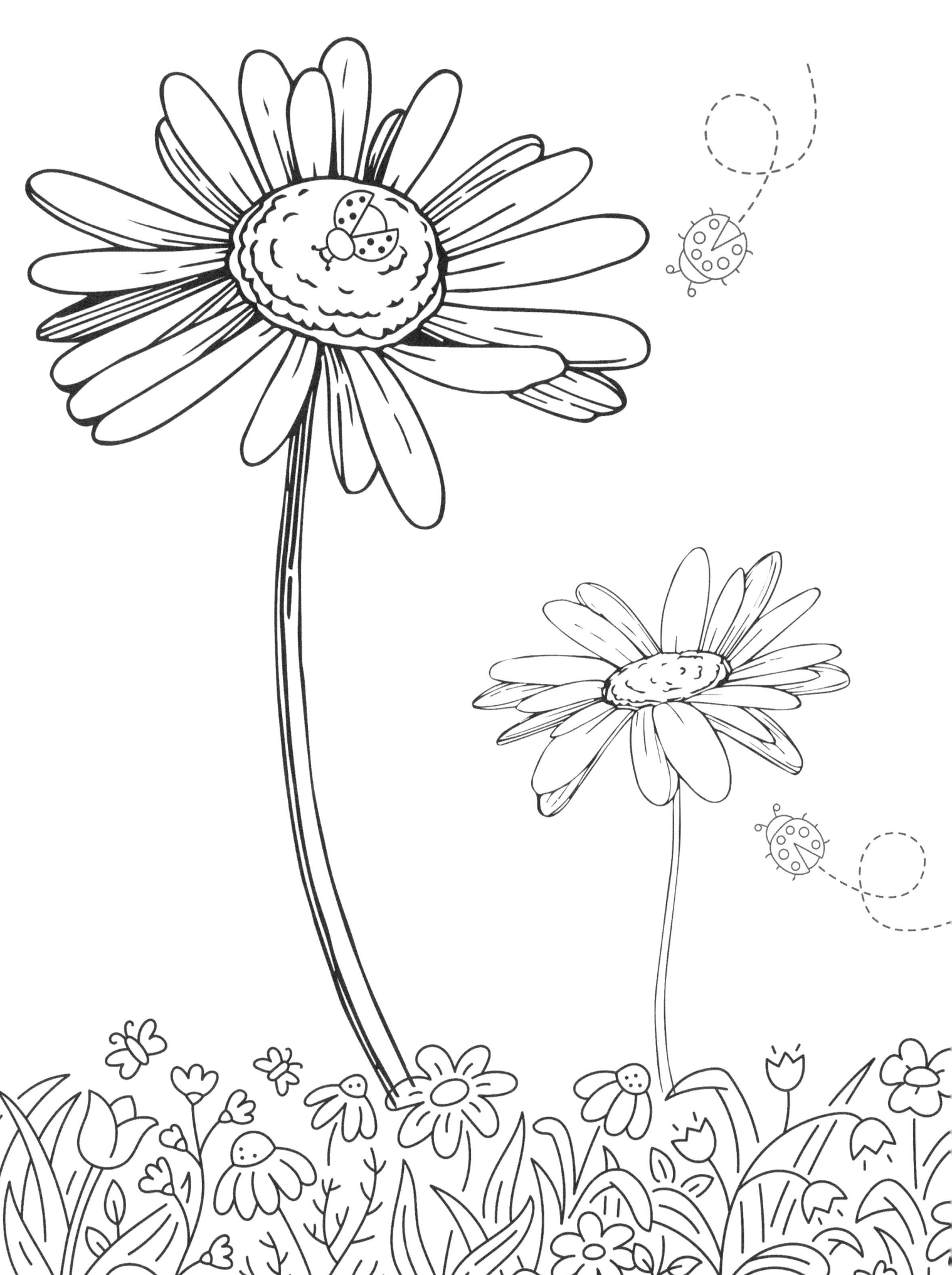

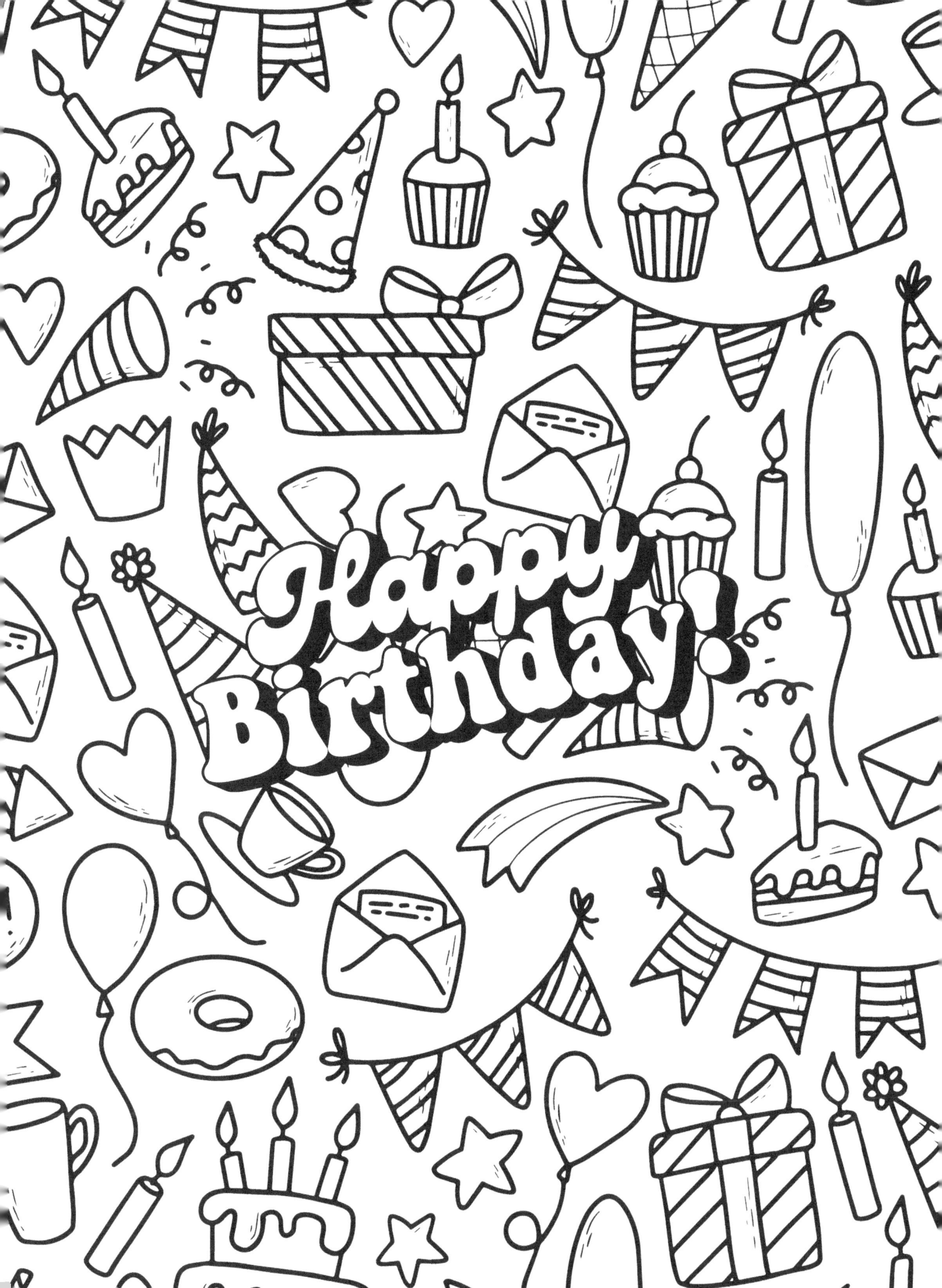

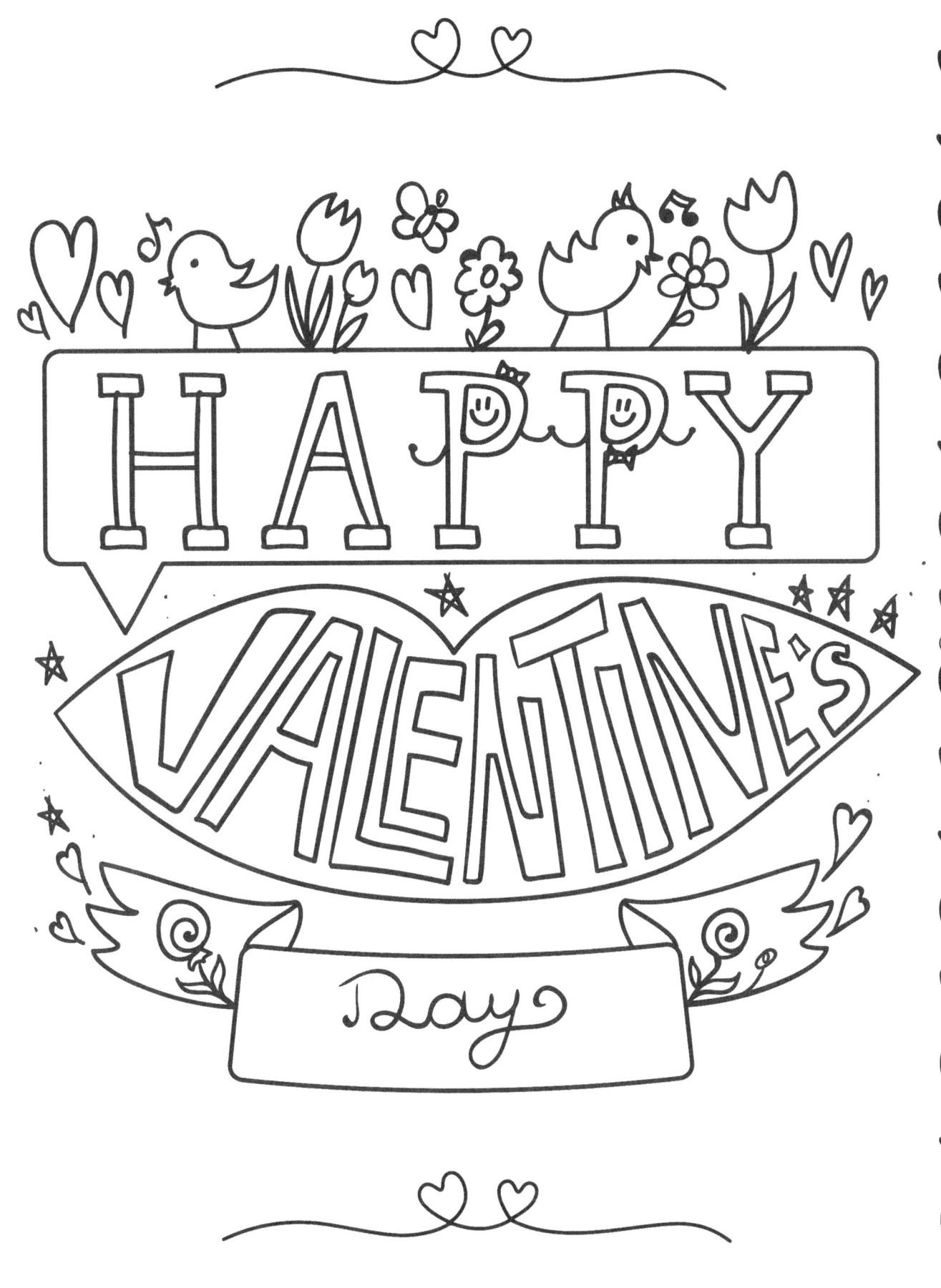

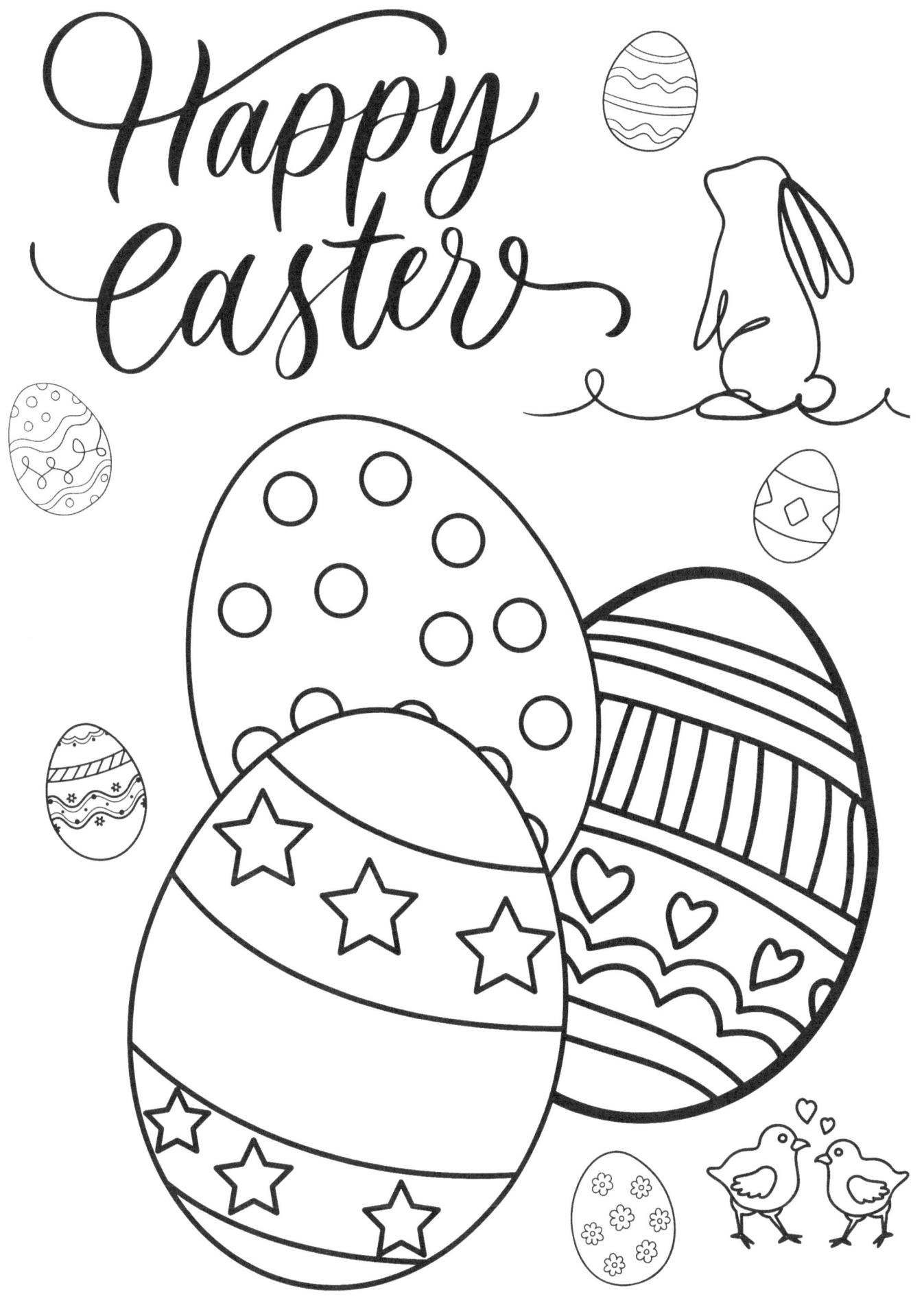

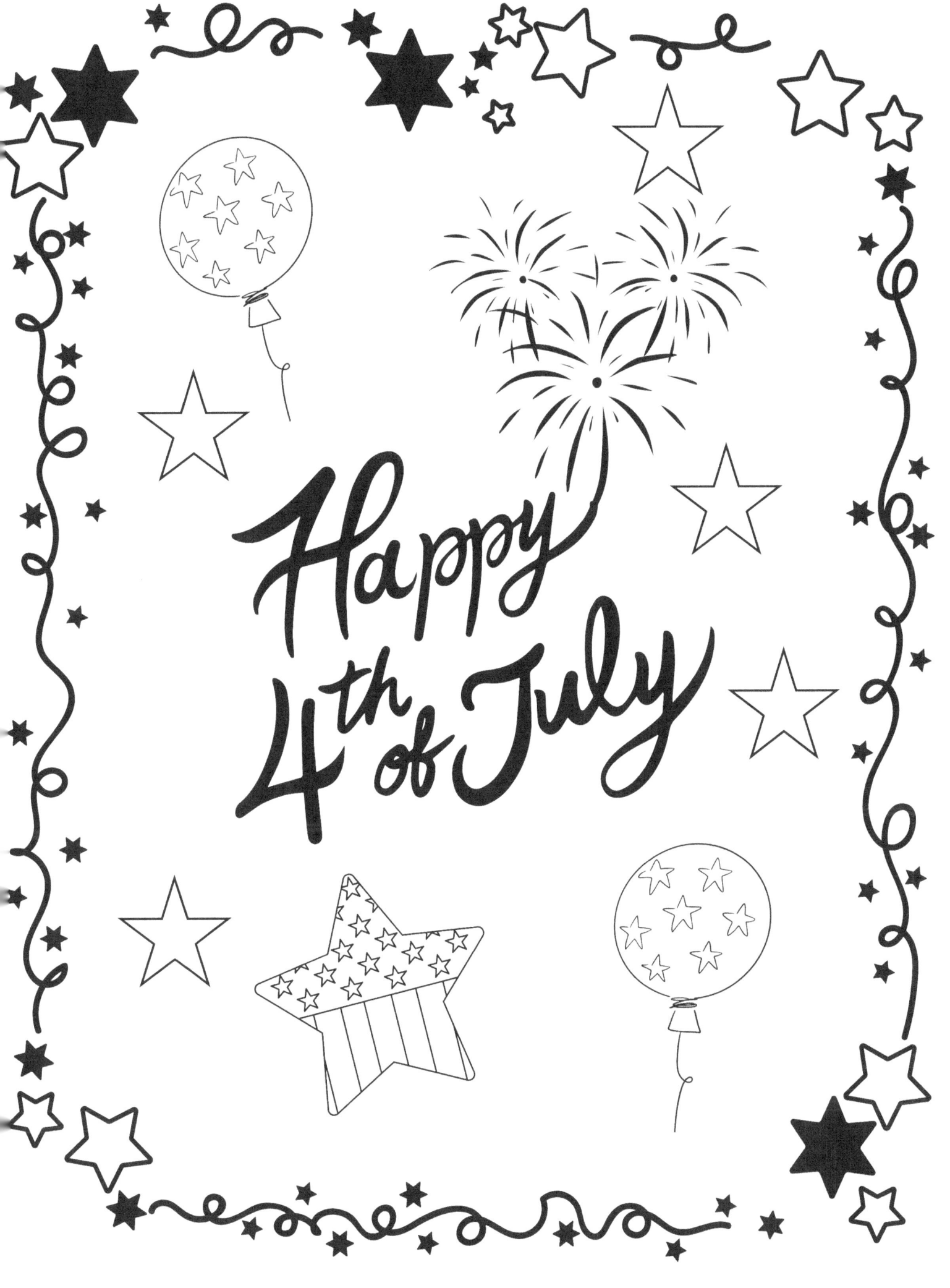

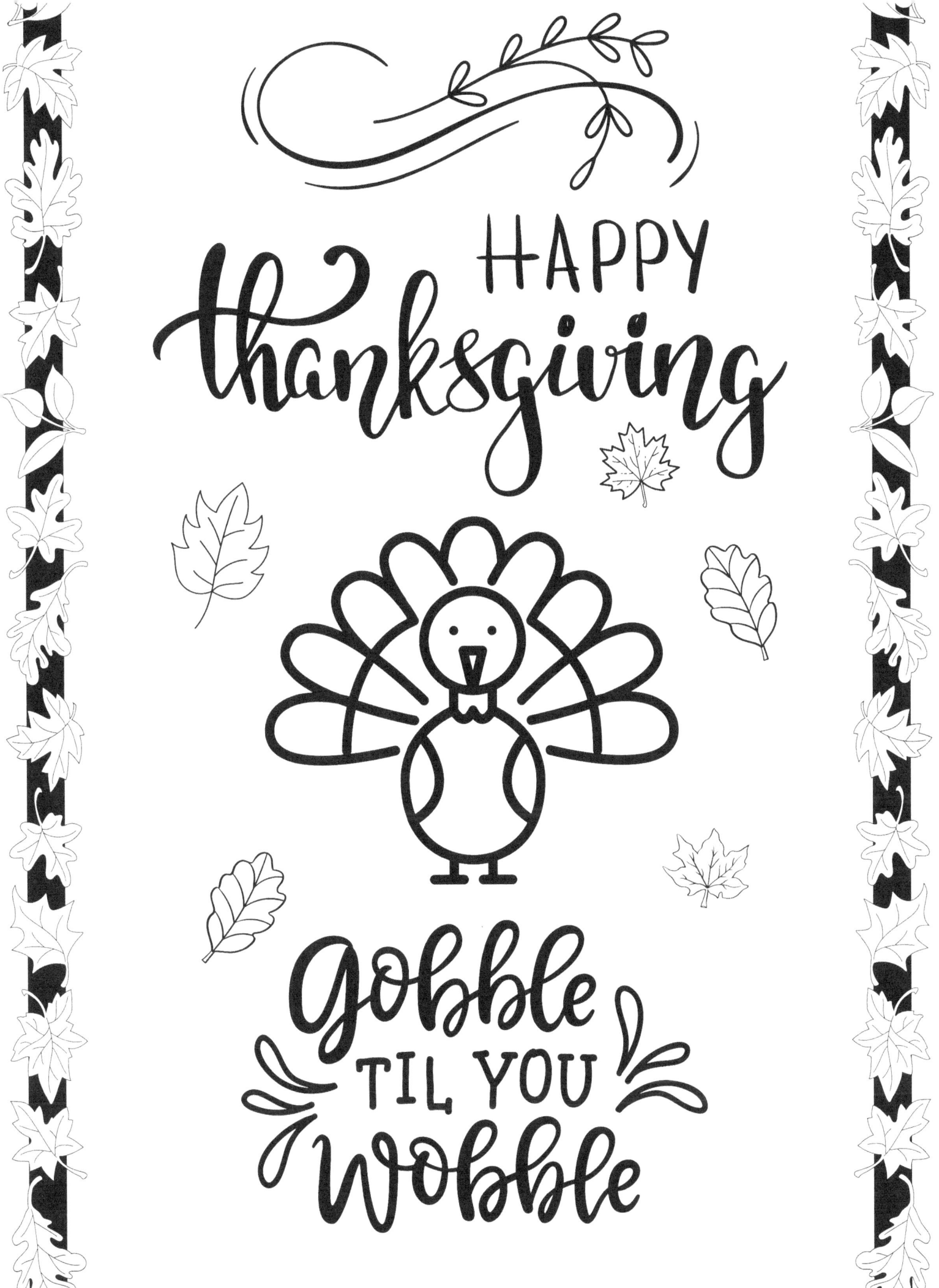

MERRY CHRISTMAS

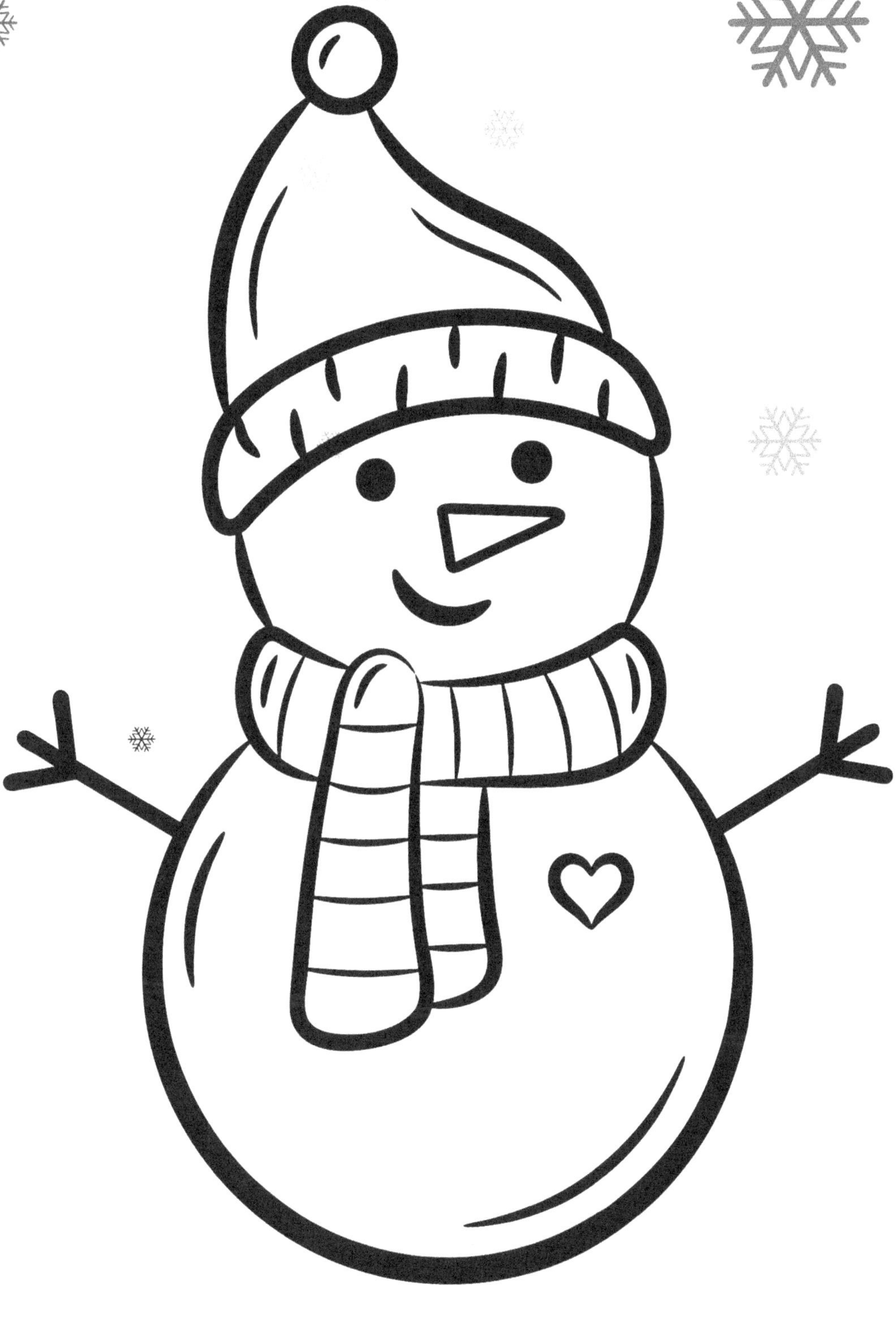

 Let it Snow

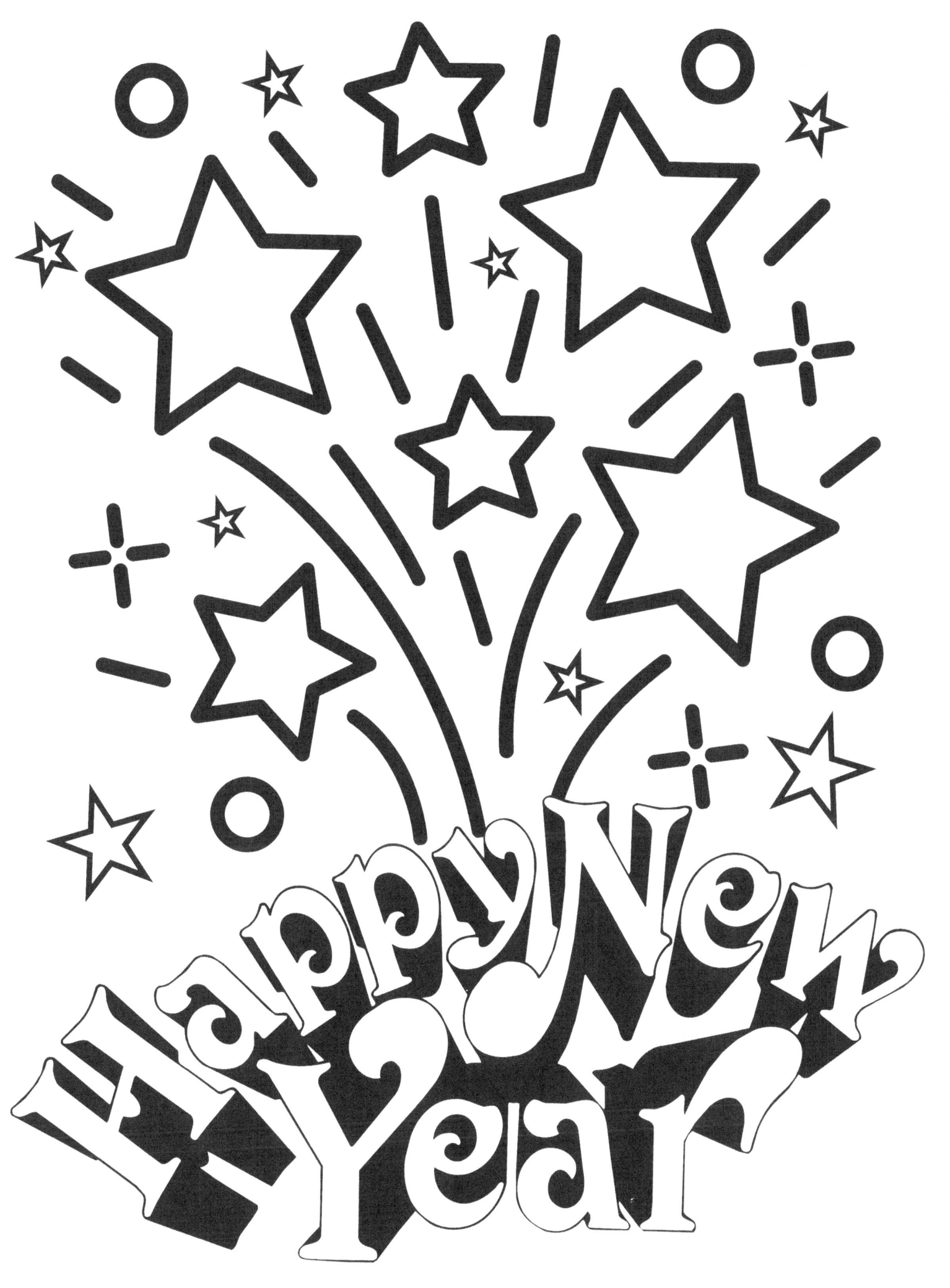

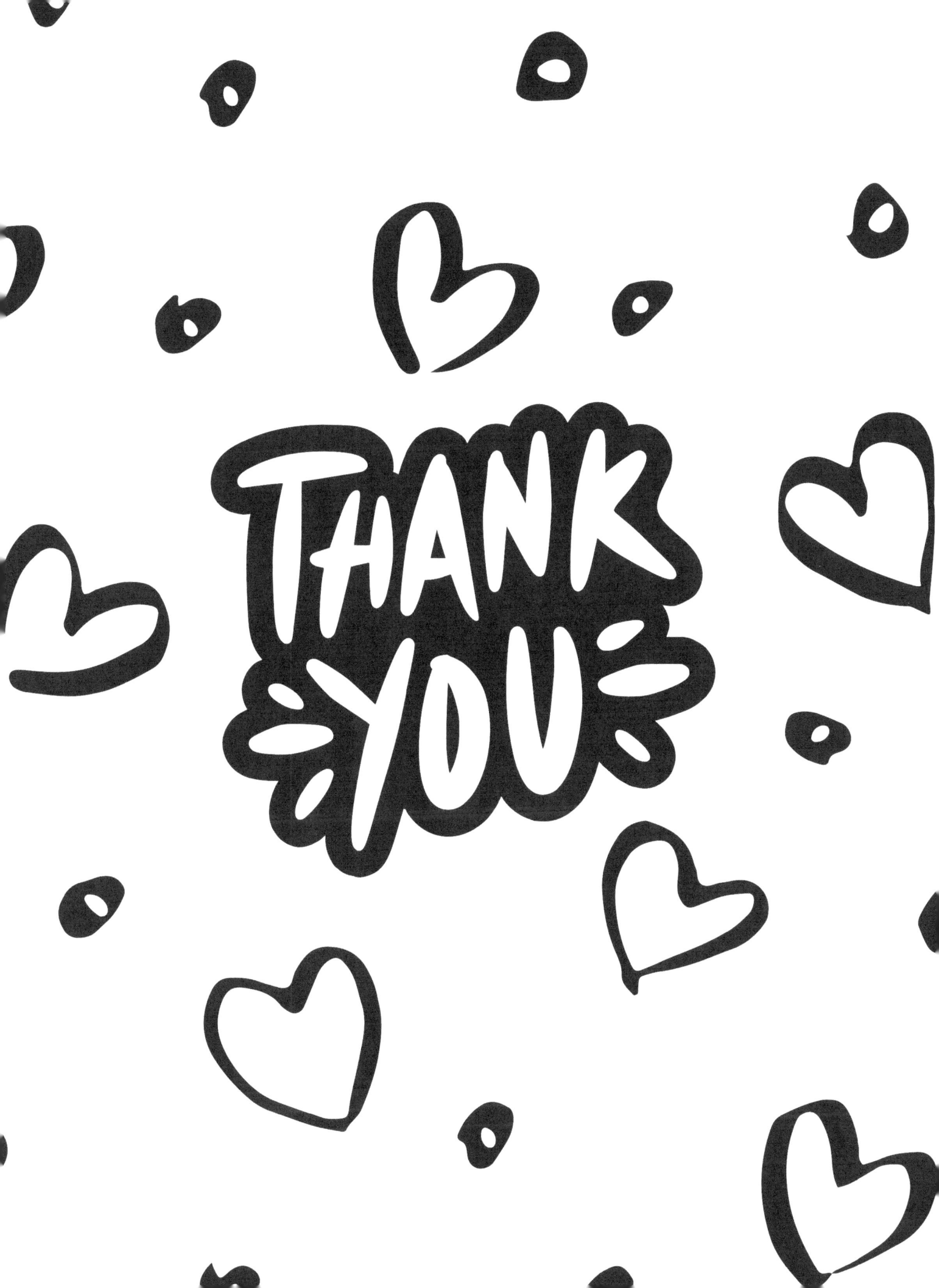

www.ingramcontent.com/pod-product-compliance
Lightning Source LLC
Chambersburg PA
CBHW080510220526
45465CB00006B/2441